The Pocket Mentor for Game Artists

Want to work as a game artist in the video game industry? Then this is the book for you. It's packed with practical advice and essential insights to help you understand how the industry works and how to get your foot in the door.

This book covers everything from choosing a specialization and building a portfolio to networking, applying for jobs, and thriving in a studio environment. It also offers advice on handling feedback, dealing with rejection, and staying healthy and competitive in a fast-paced industry.

Featuring interviews with professional game artists across multiple disciplines, this book provides real-world perspectives on different roles, career paths, and day-to-day studio life. You'll also find advice on self-assessment, training options, art tests, interviews, contracts, long-term growth, and more.

This book will be of great interest to all aspiring game artists and students of game art. It will also appeal to industry professionals looking for new ways to approach their career development.

The Pocket Mentors for Games Careers Series

The Pocket Mentors for Games Careers provide the essential information and guidance needed to get and keep a job in the modern games industry. They explain in simple, clear language exactly what a beginner needs to know about education requirements, finding job opportunities, applying for roles, and acing studio interviews. Readers will learn how to navigate studio hierarchies, transfer roles and companies, work overseas, and develop their skills.

The Pocket Mentor for Video Game Writers
Anna Megill

The Pocket Mentor for Video Game Testing
Harún Ali

The Pocket Mentor for Game Community Management
Carolin Wendt

The Pocket Mentor for Animators
Hollie Newsham

The Pocket Mentor for Game Audio
Greg Lester and Jonny Sands

The Pocket Mentor for Video Game UX UI
Simon Brewer

The Pocket Mentor for Game Production
Doug Pennant

The Pocket Mentor for Careers in VFX
David Ferreira

The Pocket Mentor for Game Artists
Sander Flisijn

For more information about this series, please visit: https://www.routledge.com/The-Pocket-Mentors-for-Games-Careers/book-series/PMGC

The Pocket Mentor for Game Artists

Sander Flisijn

CRC Press
Taylor & Francis Group
Boca Raton London New York

CRC Press is an imprint of the
Taylor & Francis Group, an **informa** business

Designed cover image: Sander Flisijn

First edition published 2026
by CRC Press
2385 NW Executive Center Drive, Suite 320, Boca Raton FL 33431

and by CRC Press
4 Park Square, Milton Park, Abingdon, Oxon, OX14 4RN

CRC Press is an imprint of Taylor & Francis Group, LLC

ISBN: 9781032794846 (hbk)
ISBN: 9781032785585 (pbk)
ISBN: 9781003492320 (ebk)

DOI: 10.1201/9781003492320

Typeset in Times
by Apex CoVantage, LLC

Dedicated to my mom, dad, brother, and partner – your love, patience, and support carried me through this. And to my two cats, who contributed by walking across my keyboardddddddddd

Contents

Acknowledgments   xiii
Copyright and Attribution   xv
Contributors   xvii
About the Author   xix
Introduction   xxi

1 Where Do I Start?   **1**
   1.1   Self-awareness   1
   1.2   Set Career Goals   2
   1.3   Create an Action Plan   3
   1.4   Take Action   4
   1.5   Evaluate Your Progress   6

2 The Video Game Industry   **7**
   2.1   The Evolution of Video Games   7
   2.2   Types of Game Studios   8
          2.2.1   Triple-A   8
          2.2.2   Indie   8
          2.2.3   Mobile   8
          2.2.4   VR/AR   9
          2.2.5   Serious and Educational   9
          2.2.6   Outsourcing   9
   2.3   The Game Development Phases   9
          2.3.1   Planning   10
          2.3.2   Pre-production   11
          2.3.3   Production   12
          2.3.4   Pre-launch   13
          2.3.5   Launch   13
          2.3.6   Post-launch   14
   2.4   Common Roles   14
          2.4.1   Publisher   15
          2.4.2   Producers   15
          2.4.3   Human Resources   15

	2.4.4	Game Designers	15
	2.4.5	Programmers	16
	2.4.6	Artists	16
	2.4.7	Animators	16
	2.4.8	Sound Designers	16
	2.4.9	Writers	17
	2.4.10	QA	17
2.5	Seniority Levels		17
	2.5.1	Junior	19
	2.5.2	Mid-level	19
	2.5.3	Senior	19
	2.5.4	Principal	20
	2.5.5	Lead	20
	2.5.6	Art Director	20
	2.5.7	Creative Director	21
2.6	Art Team Structure		21
	2.6.1	Centralized Leadership	21
	2.6.2	Discipline-Specific Leadership	23
	2.6.3	Global Leadership	23
2.7	The Harsh Reality of Game Development		25
	2.7.1	Competitive Landscape and Demand	25
	2.7.2	Crunch Culture and Burnout	25
	2.7.3	Project Cancellations	26
	2.7.4	Studio Closures and Layoffs	26
	2.7.5	Why It's Still a Rewarding Career	27

3	**Specializations**	**29**
3.1	Concept Artist	29
3.2	2D Artist	31
3.3	Character Artist	33
3.4	Environment Artist	35
3.5	Prop Artist	38
3.6	Hard-Surface Artist	40
3.7	Material Artist	43
3.8	Lighting Artist	46
3.9	Level Artist	48
3.10	Animator	50
3.11	VFX Artist	53
3.12	UI Artist	55
3.13	Cinematic Artist	57
3.14	Technical Artist	60
3.15	Generalist	63

4 Education and Training   **65**
  4.1   Degree Programs and Institutions   65
      4.1.1   Research   67
      4.1.2   Open Days   68
      4.1.3   Reach Out to Graduates   69
  4.2   Internships and Graduate Schemes   69
  4.3   Self-driven Learning   70
  4.4   Personal Projects   71
  4.5   Communities and Platforms   72
      4.5.1   Mentorship and Career Development   72
      4.5.2   Course Platforms and Tutorials   73
      4.5.3   Art Resource Marketplaces   74
      4.5.4   Industry Insight and Inspiration   74
      4.5.5   Showcase and Discovery Platforms   75
      4.5.6   Communities and Feedback Hubs   76
      4.5.7   Social and Live Communities   77

5 Feedback   **79**
  5.1   Taking Feedback   79
  5.2   Providing Feedback   80
      5.2.1   Different Ways to Provide Feedback   81
  5.3   Sharing Your Work   82
  5.4   Attachment   83

6 Networking and Events   **85**
  6.1   Game Conferences and Events   85
      6.1.1   General Conferences   85
      6.1.2   Artist-Focused Events   87
  6.2   Local Meetups   88
  6.3   Online Communities   89
  6.4   Game Jams   89
  6.5   Networking Advice   90
      6.5.1   Be Yourself   90
      6.5.2   Be Approachable   91
      6.5.3   Overcoming Anxiety   91
      6.5.4   Communication   92
      6.5.5   Quality over Quantity   92
      6.5.6   Online Networking   92
      6.5.7   Helping Others   92
      6.5.8   Business Cards   93
      6.5.9   Handling Rejection or Disinterest   93

	6.5.10	Respecting Boundaries	94
	6.5.11	Following Up	94

7 Building a Portfolio **95**
7.1 What to Include   95
7.2 Presenting Your Work   96
7.3 Where to Host Your Portfolio   98

8 Finding a Job **101**
8.1 Where and How   101
    8.1.1 Relocating for Work   101
    8.1.2 Remote Versus Office Work   102
    8.1.3 Freelancing   104
8.2 Where to Find Jobs   105
8.3 Understanding Job Listings   106
8.4 Talent Acquisition   108
8.5 Recruitment Agencies   109

9 Applying for a Job **111**
9.1 CV (Résumé)   111
    9.1.1 Additional CV Considerations   114
9.2 Cover Letter   115
9.3 Keywords and ATS   117
9.4 Leveraging Referrals   118
9.5 Art Tests   118

10 The Interview **121**
10.1 Types of Interviews   121
    10.1.1 In-Person Interviews   121
    10.1.2 Virtual Interviews   122
    10.1.3 Informal Interviews   122
10.2 Interview Preparations   122
    10.2.1 Research the Company   123
    10.2.2 Prepare Answers   124
    10.2.3 Prepare Questions   126
    10.2.4 Mock Interviews   127
10.3 NDAs   127

10.4	Mastering the Interview	128
	10.4.1 Be Yourself	128
	10.4.2 Be on Time	128
	10.4.3 Body Language	129
	10.4.4 Taking Feedback	129
	10.4.5 Presenting Your Work	130
	10.4.6 Dress Code	130
	10.4.7 Communication	130
	10.4.8 Adding Value	131
	10.4.9 Closing Strong	131
10.5	What's Next?	132

11	**Dealing with Rejection**	**133**
11.1	Don't Take It Personally	133
11.2	Stay Professional	134
11.3	Ask for Feedback	134
11.4	Analyze and Improve	135
11.5	Keep Applying	135
11.6	Staying the Course	136

12	**Contracts and Salary**	**137**
12.1	Salary Expectations	137
12.2	Negotiation	140
12.3	Types of Contracts	141
	12.3.1 Fixed-Term	142
	12.3.2 Full-Time	142
12.4	Getting Ready to Start	142

13	**Working as a Game Artist: Day-to-Day**	**145**
13.1	Studio Environment	145
13.2	Typical Workday	146
13.3	Meetings	147
	13.3.1 Core Development	147
	13.3.2 Problem-Solving and Iteration	148
	13.3.3 Studio Milestones and Syncs	148
	13.3.4 Personal Growth and Development	148
	13.3.5 External Collaboration	149
13.4	Task Management	149

13.5   Working Under Deadlines   149
13.6   Working with Other Departments   150
13.7   File Naming and Organization   151
       13.7.1 Version Control   152
13.8   Equipment   153
13.9   Software and Tools   153
       13.9.1 Communication   154
       13.9.2 Tracking and Management   155
       13.9.3 Game Engines   157
       13.9.4 Digital Content Creation   158
       13.9.5 Licensing   162
13.10 Policies and Agreements   162
       13.10.1 Probation Period   162
       13.10.2 Non-disclosure Agreement   163
       13.10.3 Creative Rights   163
       13.10.4 Non-compete Clause   164

14 Taking Care of Yourself   165
14.1   Disclaimer   165
14.2   Overtime   165
14.3   Burnout   167
14.4   Mental Health   168
14.5   Physical Health   169
       14.5.1 Ergonomics   170
14.6   Impostor Syndrome   172
14.7   Creative Blocks   173
14.8   External Organizations   173

15 What's Next?   175
15.1   Career Progression   175
15.2   Moving On   176
       15.2.1 Exit Strategy   177
15.3   Continuing to Grow   178

Closing Words   181

Acknowledgments

I would like to sincerely thank Skillsearch and Safe In Our World for their support and permission to include selected charts and data. I'm also grateful to the creator of the Game Industry Layoff Tracker for allowing the use of data from the site. I deeply appreciate the work each of them does to support the games industry and its people.

Special thanks to Will Bateman and Alyss Barraza at Taylor & Francis for their steady guidance and support throughout the development of this book. Their involvement made this experience both rewarding and memorable, and I'm grateful to have had their partnership in bringing this project to life.

Copyright and Attribution

Contributors

This book draws heavily from my personal experience and knowledge – from being a student, to mentoring others, to working my way up and becoming a lead. While I've packed as much insight into these pages as I can, no one person knows everything about every aspect of this industry. Game art is a broad field, and there are many specializations within it.

So, in order to give you a broader and more well-rounded perspective, I've interviewed several incredible professional game artists from various disciplines, each bringing their own unique background and experiences. You'll find their insights in Chapter 3, "Specializations," along with highlighted quotes from them throughout the book.

My sincere thanks to the following contributors, listed in alphabetical order:

- **Damian Audino** (Freelance Concept Artist)
  https://www.artstation.com/damianaudino
- **Etienne Bednarz** (Senior Material Specialist/Environment Artist)
  https://www.artstation.com/wenceslas
- **Quinn Bogaerts** (3D Prop Artist)
  https://www.artstation.com/quinnbogaerts
- **Geoffroy Calis** (Senior Lighting Artist at Remedy Entertainment)
  https://www.artstation.com/geoffroycalis
- **Edd Coates** (Lead UI/UX Artist and Designer)
  https://www.gameuidatabase.com/
- **Julian Elwood** (Senior Environment Artist at Naughty Dog)
  https://www.artstation.com/elwoodvii
- **Oliver Elm** (Senior 2D Artist/Narrative Designer)
- **Florian Guillaud** (Senior VFX Artist at DON'T NOD)
  https://www.artstation.com/florianguillaud
- **Joyce Makker** (Associate Director of Gameplay Animation at Hangar 13)
- **Shona Markusen** (Cinematic Artist)
  https://www.linkedin.com/in/shonamarkusen
- **Dylan Mellott** (Senior 3D Hard Surface Artist)
  https://www.artstation.com/dmellott11

- **Juan Novelletto** (Senior Character Artist)
  https://juannovelletto.artstation.com/
- **Philippe Routhier** (Senior Level Artist)
  https://www.artstation.com/prouthier
- **Mohsen Tabasi** (Senior Technical Artist at Splash Damage)
  https://mohsen-t.artstation.com/

About the Author

Sander Flisijn is a Lead Character Artist with over a decade of professional experience in the games industry. He began his career at a game studio before earning his bachelor's degree in visual arts and has since worked across both indie and AAA studios. He has contributed to a variety of titles, including *Cronos: The New Dawn*, *Mafia III*, *Mafia: Definitive Edition*, and *Borderlands: Game of the Year Enhanced Edition*.

In addition to his work on games, Sander has created highly regarded 3D modeling courses, praised for their clarity and depth. He also shares his expertise through career talks and hands-on workshops focused on game art and professional growth.

Introduction

Hello, and welcome! First off, thank you for picking up this book. If you're reading this, there's a good chance you're passionate about games and considering a career as a game artist. That's a pretty exciting direction to be heading in. The video game industry is one of the biggest and fastest-growing entertainment sectors in the world, but it's also highly competitive and challenging to break into. This book is here to guide, inspire, and support you.

However, before we go any further, I want to make one thing clear: this book isn't about teaching you how to draw, sculpt, or paint better. If you're looking for techniques to improve your skills in game art, there are plenty of great resources out there – and I encourage you to seek them out. What this book is about is equally important: building a career as a game artist. If you're looking to understand what it takes to enter the industry, stay motivated, and keep growing, you're in the right place.

Now, when it comes to game art, it's more than just beautiful visuals – it's a fundamental part of how players experience and judge a game. While gameplay is important, it's the visuals that usually make the first impression. It's often said you shouldn't judge a book by its cover, yet most of us do – and the same goes for games. A player can't feel how a game plays until they've already decided to give it a try, and that decision is often made based on how the game looks.

This makes game art a unique discipline within game development, with its own specific demands and challenges. Unlike static images or animated films – where each frame can be pre-rendered to perfection – game assets need to work in real time, often on limited hardware. This adds an extra layer of complexity, requiring game artists to balance their creative vision with technical limitations like performance, optimization, and engine constraints.

As the industry continues to evolve, so does game art. With new tools and technologies constantly pushing the boundaries, artists must stay on top of both the creative and technical sides of their work if they want to keep up.

But here's the reality: breaking into the industry as an artist isn't just about learning how to make great art. It's very much about strategy, too. Sure, your artistic and technical skills are the foundation, but building a career in game art takes more than just being good at what you do. From understanding the different specializations you might pursue to building a strong portfolio and navigating your career path, this book will guide you through every step, providing you with the information needed to take actionable steps toward your goals.

By the time you finish this book, I hope you'll have the knowledge and confidence to take on the industry. I can't promise that this book will make you an expert overnight, but I do promise that if you put in the work, you'll be well on your way.

With that in mind, let's get started!

Where Do I Start?

1

You can't board a rocket without knowing where you're headed. Just as a successful space mission requires careful planning, so does your career. I know it can be intimidating not knowing where to start, but following a structured approach is what gets your mission off the ground.

In this chapter, we'll go over the steps to help you launch your career with clarity. The first step is to figure out where you are, what skills you currently have, and where you want to go. After you have that clarity, we can pinpoint your career goals and develop a plan of action to help you reach them.

1.1 SELF-AWARENESS

If you're not aware of what's holding you back, it's hard to make progress. That's where self-awareness comes in. It's more than just knowing where you are right now or what skills you have – it's about recognizing the habits, challenges, and circumstances that could shape your path moving forward.

Each of us has a unique set of conditions that impact our journey. Things like where you live can make a significant difference in the job opportunities and education that are available to you. Your finances or personal commitments, like family, part-time work, or other responsibilities, can affect how much time and energy you can put into your career development. And let's not forget, your mental and physical well-being also play an important role in how effectively you will be able to chase your goals.

Of course, there are certain things in life we have no control over – like where we were born, unexpected setbacks, or health conditions. So instead, focus on what you *can* control. Work on preparing yourself, practicing, and constantly improving so that when opportunities come knocking, you're ready to seize them.

Now, take a moment and think about where you're at right now. What skills and knowledge do you already have? More importantly, how do these align with the direction you want to go in?

DOI: 10.1201/9781003492320-1

1

For instance, let's say your goal is to become an environment artist. Maybe you're already confident in your 3D modeling but feel like you need to work on your texturing skills. Recognizing both your strengths and weaknesses helps you identify what to focus on next.

This kind of self-assessment is where real progress starts. It gives you a clearer picture of what you need to learn, what projects to take on, and where to invest your time. What matters most is that you're honest with yourself about where you stand and where you want to go.

Think of self-awareness not as a one-time exercise but as an ongoing habit. It's something you'll need to keep doing as you grow. Your goals and circumstances will shift over time, and being aware of those changes will help you stay on track and adjust when needed.

But before any of that can happen, you need to know where you're headed. You need to set a clear goal you care about. That's the starting point for everything that follows.

> *"Think about what you want in the future. What will get you there? In your present circumstances, focus on that."*
>
> – Oliver Elm

1.2 SET CAREER GOALS

Goals are like a compass; they give you direction, purpose, and a way to measure how far you've come. With a clear goal in mind, you can focus your energy on making progress, step by step. Without a goal, it can be easy to feel lost or distracted.

The first step is figuring out what excites you about game art. There are so many paths to explore: character and environment art, animation, visual effects (VFX), or user interface (UI) design, to name a few. Are you drawn to something specific – like creating immersive environments or designing epic characters? Or maybe you want to be a generalist, doing a bit of everything? What about freelancing, where you call the shots?

And here's the thing – it's okay if you don't know yet. When I first started, I wasn't sure either. Back in school, I thought, *why not try everything?* That curiosity helped me discover that I love working on characters the most. Your goals don't have to be set in stone. They'll evolve as you learn and grow, and that's part of the process.

Let me tell you a secret: no one has their entire career mapped out from the start. The important thing is to stay curious and keep moving forward. Don't let the unknown hold you back. In Chapter 3, we'll dive deeper into the most common specializations for game artists, and by the end of this book, you'll have a much clearer idea of which path best matches your interests and skills.

To help you get started defining your career goal(s), here are some questions to think about:

• What excites me most about game art? Is it characters, environments, VFX, or something else entirely?
• Is there a specific game genre or art style I'm drawn to?
• What kinds of projects would I love to work on?
• What skills do I already have, and what do I need to learn to get where I want to go?
• How much time can I dedicate to improving my skills?
• Would I prefer working in a big team on large projects or at a smaller, more independent studio?
• What kind of work environment feels right for me – in a studio, remotely, or in a hybrid setup?
• Am I open to relocating for a job?

There's no right or wrong answer. Just take the time to explore what feels right for you. Starting with these questions can help you uncover what drives you, and from there, you'll be ready to create a plan to make it happen.

1.3 CREATE AN ACTION PLAN

Once you've defined your long-term career goal, the next step is turning that vision into a concrete path forward – and that's where an action plan comes in. Think of it as the bridge between where you are now and where you want to be. What steps do you need to take? What's your strategy? And how long will it all take? An action plan is just that: a breakdown of steps (the *actions* or short-term goals, as we'll call them) and the strategy (the *plan*) to get them done.

When I set out to become a character artist, I thought to myself: if my long-term goal is to create characters for games, I need to understand what it takes to be a character artist. So, I did my homework. I studied the portfolios of accomplished character artists, listened to podcasts and interviews to soak up information, and analyzed job descriptions to pinpoint exactly what studios were looking for.

That research gave me a clear roadmap of what to focus on. I broke my long-term goal into smaller, actionable steps (short-term goals) that I could tackle one at a time. Each short-term goal felt manageable, and together, they brought me closer to where I wanted to be.

Here's the thing: an action plan keeps you moving toward your goals. Without one, it's like heading out on a road trip without a map. Sure, you might stumble your way to your destination, but it's far more likely you'll get lost along the way.

So, how do you create an action plan? Start with the end in mind. Define your long-term goal clearly, and then find out what it takes to get there. Don't worry about the order just yet. Just get everything down that comes to mind.

For instance, if your goal is to become a character artist, your list might include learning anatomy, getting better at 3D sculpting, building a portfolio, and enrolling in a mentorship or game art course. If that course is in another city or country, break down what steps are needed to make that move possible. Be specific.

Once you've listed your short-term goals, think about the order in which they should be tackled. Creating a timeline can be helpful here: a simple visual with today's date on one end and your long-term goal's deadline on the other. Then, plot each short-term goal along the timeline based on how long it will take to complete and how it connects to other steps. For example, it makes more sense to first study basic anatomy and proportions – starting with individual body parts like the head, hands, or torso – before attempting to sculpt a full human figure. By breaking it down this way, your plan becomes not just a list but a logical progression.

Don't worry about making it fancy. Your action plan will do just fine on a calendar, a whiteboard, sticky notes, or a Trello board – whatever works best for you. I've been living in front of a whiteboard myself while writing this book. Just make sure you write it down somewhere. Seeing your plan laid out in front of you makes it easier to stay focused, motivated, and accountable.

At the end of the day, it's all about consistent progress. One step at a time. With a clear plan and steady effort, you'll get where you want to go.

1.4 TAKE ACTION

Setting goals and creating an action plan are just the first steps. If you want to make real progress, you've got to put in the work. Without putting in the work, even the best plan means nothing. And yes, that often means making sacrifices. Maybe you skip an episode of your favorite TV show, turn down a game night with friends, or get up early on the weekend. But the hours you put in now will pay off in the long run. Of course, I'm not telling you to ditch your downtime entirely. Balance matters, and we'll get to that shortly.

When you start something new, you're probably going to suck at it first. That's just how it works. Whether you're trying to learn a new skill or take on a new project – those early days can be tough. You'll likely feel frustrated when you compare your work to the impressive artworks of experienced artists. I remember feeling like my work was far from where I wanted it to be as I scrolled through incredible portfolios, convinced mine didn't measure up.

But here's where persistence becomes your best friend. The secret to pushing past that early frustration is repetition. The more you practice, the better you get. Your first attempts might fall short, but each one is progress. With every try, you're learning, improving, and narrowing the gap between where you are and where you want to be.

The focus isn't on perfection (because let's be real, perfection is a never-ending chase, even for the best of us). The goal is progress. Improvement happens with time and effort, and one day, you'll look back and be amazed at how far you've come.

Honestly, I wasn't great when I started. But I knew what "good" looked like, and that clarity made all the difference. I wasn't where I wanted to be, but I could see the direction I needed to go. Unfortunately, many beginners don't have that perspective, which can hold them back. So here's my advice: study the work of professionals. Aim for that level of quality. If you want to land a job as a game artist, that's the level you need to reach. But as I mentioned before, and I'll repeat it here: focus on making progress rather than aiming for perfection. You won't hit that level overnight, but with consistent effort, you can get there too.

Also, understand that productivity isn't a straight line. Some days, you'll feel unstoppable, crossing off your to-do list like a machine. On other days, you might get just one small task done. That's okay. The important part is consistency. Keep showing up, keep putting in the work, and even on those slower days, progress will come.

Motivation plays a huge role in this process. To stay motivated, you need to feed your mind with inspiration. A quick scroll through ArtStation or listening to a podcast while sipping on your coffee could give you that much-needed boost of inspiration. Just make sure that inspiration pushes you into action. It's not enough to feel inspired – you need to do something with that energy.

Passion helps, too. It's what drives us to work harder and push through challenges. However, passion alone isn't enough. You need to give yourself space to rest, too. As cliché as it sounds, it's true: the journey to reaching your career goals isn't a sprint; it's a marathon.

You might feel guilty for taking breaks. I've felt it too, and taking breaks from writing this very book was no exception. But here's what I've learned: rest isn't a weakness. It's a requirement. Overworking leads to burnout, and burnout will suck your motivation dry. It's okay to take a step back to enjoy a hobby, spend time with family or friends, or simply reset for a bit. In fact, it can actually help you come back more focused, recharged, and ready to see things more clearly.

Achieving your career goals isn't a straight path. There will be detours, setbacks, and obstacles along the way. I've faced plenty myself. But you know what? Each one made me more focused and determined on my goals. So keep going. Learn from your mistakes. Keep putting in the work. And step by step, you'll get closer to where you want to be.

> *"Make the things you like and a lot of it. The rest will come naturally."*
> – Dylan Mellott

1.5 EVALUATE YOUR PROGRESS

Evaluating your progress is the last step, but it's just as important. You need to look back and see how far you've come to stay motivated and focused. Here's a trick that always works: compare your current work to what you did weeks or months ago. Day-to-day changes might seem small, but when you step back and see the bigger picture, you'll realize just how much you've grown. It's easy to get caught up in the grind and feel like you're not making progress, but trust me, you are.

Taking time to reflect on what's working and what isn't is how you grow. Your action plan isn't set in stone – it's a living, breathing document that needs regular check-ins. As you tick off tasks, pause to assess if you're still on track. If something isn't working, don't hesitate to adjust. Maybe your schedule needs tweaking, or a particular task requires more focus. Just as your skills evolve, so will your goals. What you want now might change in five years, and that's okay.

If one path turns out not to be what you thought it would be – say, specializing in animation – that's a signal to explore new directions. Your action plan should be flexible enough to adapt to these shifts.

So, keep your plan clear and adaptable, and above all, keep moving forward. Sometimes, a small change today can lead to big wins tomorrow.

The Video Game Industry

2

Now that you've learned how to set clear goals and build an action plan to guide your progress, it's time to zoom out and look at the bigger picture – the video game industry itself.

If you're on the path to becoming a game artist, it's important to understand how the industry works. The more you know, the better you'll be at steering your career where you want it to go.

2.1 THE EVOLUTION OF VIDEO GAMES

But first, let's take a quick trip back to the 1970s, the time when video games made their first mark with arcade games and home consoles. Games like *Pong* (1972) and *Space Invaders* (1978) were simple but groundbreaking. Most of the time, they were made by small teams or even solo developers, who had to do a bit of everything. And while they look basic now, those early titles laid the foundation for everything that followed.

Then came the 1980s and 1990s, often referred to as the "gaming boom." Technology was advancing fast. Consoles like the NES (1983) and Sega Genesis (1989) brought gaming into people's living rooms. Games got bigger, bolder, and more ambitious. Think *Super Mario Bros.* (1985), *The Legend of Zelda* (1986), and *Street Fighter II* (1991). New genres and gameplay mechanics were born and shaped the modern gaming landscape we know today.

Not only did the games become more complex, but so did the methods used to create them. Development pipelines evolved, and roles became more specialized. Artists, for example, went from being jacks-of-all-trades to becoming specialists focusing on specific things like character art, animations, and visual effects. Studios grew, and teams expanded.

DOI: 10.1201/9781003492320-2

Fast-forward to today, the video game industry has evolved into a global powerhouse. We're talking billions in revenue, teams working across continents, and roles that didn't even exist a decade ago. What once started as a hobby in someone's basement has now evolved into the world's largest entertainment sector.

It's pretty amazing to see how far video games have come and even more exciting to think about where they, and you, are headed next.

2.2 TYPES OF GAME STUDIOS

But before we look too far ahead, it's worth understanding who's driving the industry today. Game development happens across a wide range of studios, each contributing in different ways. While every studio is unique in size, focus, and scope, they generally fall into the following categories:

2.2.1 Triple-A

Triple-A (AAA) studios are large, well-resourced companies producing high-budget, blockbuster games. These studios usually have hundreds of employees and work under major publishers. Think cinematic graphics, massive marketing campaigns, and franchises like *Call of Duty* or *Assassin's Creed*.

2.2.2 Indie

Independent (indie) studios are typically small teams – or even solo developers – creating games often without the support of large publishers. They often focus on creative, niche, or experimental ideas, with limited budgets but lots of passion and freedom.

2.2.3 Mobile

Mobile game studios focus on games for smartphones and tablets. These can range from casual puzzle games to complex strategy titles. They often prioritize accessibility, short play sessions, and monetization through ads or in-app purchases.

2.2.4 VR/AR

Studios in this space develop games for virtual reality (VR) and augmented reality (AR) platforms. VR games offer fully immersive, 360-degree worlds built for headsets like the Meta Quest or Valve Index, with titles like *Beat Saber*, *Fear of Heights*, or *Half-Life: Alyx*. These experiences often blur the boundary between the digital and real worlds, prompting players to instinctively duck, dodge, or flinch as though reacting to something real.

AR studios, on the other hand, blend digital elements into the real world through devices like smartphones or AR glasses, as seen in games like *Pokémon GO* and *Harry Potter: Wizards Unite*. Both VR and AR studios sit at the cutting edge of interactive tech, often experimenting with new forms of gameplay.

2.2.5 Serious and Educational

These studios create games designed for purposes beyond entertainment – such as education, training, health care, or social impact. Whether it's helping someone learn a new language, guiding a med student through lifesaving procedures, or raising awareness about global issues like climate change. While they still use game mechanics, the primary goal is learning or behavior change rather than pure entertainment.

2.2.6 Outsourcing

Outsourcing studios specialize in providing services to other game developers. This can include art, animation, programming, QA testing, or porting games to different platforms. If you check the credits of nearly any game – whether it's an indie or AAA title – chances are you'll find that at least one outsourcing studio contributed to its development. They're a crucial part of the industry pipeline, especially for large projects with tight deadlines.

2.3 THE GAME DEVELOPMENT PHASES

Games come in all shapes and sizes – some take six months to build, while others may take several years. Despite the differences, most games follow a

Planning

Pre-Production

Production

Pre-Launch

Launch

Post-Launch

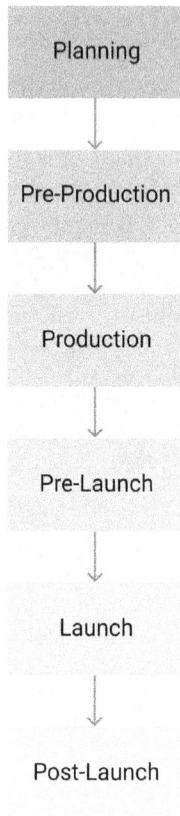

FIGURE 2.1   Overview of the game development phases.

similar development process that's become standard across the industry. Each studio might handle things a bit differently, but understanding the typical phases helps you see how a game comes together. From the initial idea all the way to launch, every step matters in making sure the smooth development and success of a game. Figure 2.1 illustrates the six key phases of this process. Let's walk through it.

2.3.1 Planning

The ancient Greek philosopher Plato believed that how something begins often shapes its entire outcome – making the early stages of any work the most crucial.[1] Well, he wasn't wrong. The planning phase is where everything kicks off. It's where a raw idea turns into a tangible vision and lays the groundwork for development.

This is when the team asks the big questions: What kind of game is this? 2D or 3D? What art style fits? What gameplay mechanics do we want? Which game engine are we using? Multiplayer? Dynamic weather? And what do the levels, characters, and assets roughly look like?

While ideas may change and evolve during development (and they always do), locking in the basics early on helps keep things on track and avoids delays or feature cuts later on.

The team also tackles the practical stuff: How long will this take? What's the budget? What resources are needed? This makes sure the project isn't just wishful thinking but something realistic and doable.

To make the plan actionable, the team creates a production schedule with key milestones (major checkpoints to track progress throughout development). To reach those milestones, work is broken into short, focused periods called sprints (typically lasting one to four weeks), where specific tasks are completed. Each sprint typically includes planning, daily stand-ups, reviews, and retrospectives to stay on track.

Planning is also when the team is assembled. Roles are assigned, and new talent is brought on. However, recruitment doesn't stop there – it usually continues throughout all phases of development.

Once the vision is clear and the plan is set, the team is ready to enter pre-production with a solid path forward.

2.3.2 Pre-production

Pre-production is often called the "heavy exploration" phase. At this point, the team knows their destination but is still figuring out how to get there.

One of the biggest parts of this phase is prototyping. This is when the team builds rough, playable versions of the game to test out the core mechanics – what's often referred to as the "proof of concept." These early builds aren't polished; they exist to experiment, identify what's fun, and refine the gameplay before heading to full production.

As gameplay takes shape, so does the broader vision. That's where the game design document (GDD) comes in. Written by designers with input from directors, writers, and producers, it outlines the game's vision, mechanics, and features. It evolves over time and serves as the project's reference point.

Two major milestones usually define the pre-production phase: the "First Playable" and the "Vertical Slice."

- **First Playable**: A basic version of the game with working core mechanics. The art is rough and placeholder, but the focus is on gameplay and functionality.
- **Vertical Slice**: A polished segment showcasing final art, sound, and gameplay. It acts as a high-quality demo and sets the standard for the rest of the game. It's like slicing a piece of the cake so you know how the whole thing will taste, hence the name Vertical Slice.

As these (and future) milestones approach, teams often set a content lock two weeks in advance to freeze major changes. This helps stabilize builds, prevents last-minute disruptions, and ensures each milestone is delivered in a testable state.

Meanwhile, the art team begins defining the visual direction. They create concept art, placeholders, and early models while setting up pipelines for later production. Sometimes, they build a "beautiful corner": a small polished area focused purely on visuals, serving as a style guide and benchmark for the whole game.

In short, pre-production is when everything starts coming together. It's about testing ideas, identifying what makes the gameplay engaging, and preparing for full production with a clear plan and vision.

2.3.3 Production

The production phase is where most of the work happens. It's the period of full-on content creation that will make up the final game. It's the longest and most demanding phase, often lasting months to several years, depending on the project's scale.

During this time, artists, designers, and programmers work in parallel. Artists turn concepts into finished models, textures, and animations. Programmers build systems and mechanics. Designers ensure all elements come together to create a fun, balanced experience that aligns with the vision.

But production isn't without challenges. Deadlines, budgets, and technical issues can cause setbacks. Teams must adapt, communicate, and solve problems quickly to stay on track.

Three major milestones define the production phase: "Pre-alpha," "Alpha," and "Beta."

- **Pre-alpha**: Most core gameplay features are in place, though the game is still rough and incomplete. It's playable but lacks polish, and the focus is on core functionality and identifying major issues.

- **Alpha**: The game is nearly feature-complete, with all major systems and content in place. It's playable from start to finish but still needs debugging and stability improvements.
- **Beta**: Most bugs are resolved, and the game is fully feature-complete. This phase focuses on final polishing before pre-launch.

In short, production is where the pieces come together. By the end, the game is ready for the pre-launch phase and, ultimately, release.

2.3.4 Pre-launch

Pre-launch is all about fine-tuning and polishing the game to ensure everything is in place before it hits the shelves.

While testing occurs during most phases of development, it intensifies during the pre-launch phase. Quality assurance (QA) plays the game repeatedly, tracking down bugs, glitches, and performance issues across all platforms.

External testers are also often brought in to offer fresh perspectives, giving feedback on balance, difficulty, and overall experience.

Since games are released globally, most undergo a localization process. This means adapting the game's text, audio, and cultural references for different languages and regions.

As the finish line nears, two major milestones are hit: "Release Candidate" and the "Gold Master."

- **Release Candidate**: A near-final version, feature-complete, and heavily tested. It may go through several iterations, as the team makes final tweaks based on feedback. The team often creates multiple release candidates, refining each based on testing feedback until one meets all criteria and becomes the Gold Master.
- **Gold Master**: The final approved version for release. This build is sent for mass production or digital upload. It's considered done, though studios may prepare a day-one patch for last-minute fixes.

In short, pre-launch is when the game reaches its final form – polished, tested, and ready for players to experience.

2.3.5 Launch

The launch phase is when all the hard work finally pays off. After months to years of development, the game is out for players to experience.

Marketing often begins well in advance, sometimes years before the game releases. Trailers drop, social campaigns ramp up, influencers get involved, and developers often hop on live streams or events to build hype.

For the development team, launch brings pride, excitement, and a bit of anxiety. It's the moment their work is shared with the world. A smooth launch can define a game's legacy, while a rocky one can leave lasting marks.

After launch, some team members might shift to new projects, while others move into the next phase: post-launch.

2.3.6 Post-launch

Launching the game doesn't mean the work is done. After release, the team monitors feedback, fixes bugs, fine-tunes the balance, and keeps servers stable. A smooth launch is great, but the real work starts once players dive in. Post-launch support is vital – not just for player satisfaction (and Metacritic scores) but for the game's long-term success.

Alongside maintenance, developers sometimes begin work on download-able content (DLC) or free updates (new levels, cosmetics, or quality-of-life features) to keep players engaged.

Post-launch is also when the team usually celebrates with a well-earned release party. Holding it after launch makes sense – during launch, as well as post-launch, a portion of the team is often still busy fixing last-minute issues or preparing patches. Waiting until the busiest stretch has passed gives everyone the chance to relax and enjoy the moment together.

But post-launch isn't only about upkeep and celebration. It's also a time for reflection. The team holds a post-mortem (Latin for "after death") to review the development process: what worked, what didn't, and how to improve. It's a chance to share insights, voice frustrations, and carry lessons forward to future projects.

2.4 COMMON ROLES

Game development is a team effort that involves a variety of roles. While many of these roles have specializations within, they all work together toward a common goal: creating a game that players will love. Let's explore the most common roles in game development, along with how each contributes to the development.

2.4.1 Publisher

The publisher is responsible for the funding, marketing, and getting the game out to the world. But it's not just about money; they also provide valuable resources and guidance to help keep the game on track and hitting all the right marks (in gameplay, technically, visually, financially, and on time). Publishers are usually external companies, but some game studios choose to self-publish without relying on external publishers. Now, publishers aren't all the same. Their level of involvement can vary from publisher to publisher. Some prefer to be heavily involved and closely monitor the development process, while others take a more hands-off approach, letting the development team lead the way.

2.4.2 Producers

Producers oversee the entire production process, making sure the game is completed on time, within budget, and to the desired quality standards. They act as the communication link between all the different departments, managing the project's schedule, coordinating teams, and prioritizing tasks to keep everything on track. Producers also handle resources like outsourcing, solve problems, and make important decisions to keep development running smoothly.

2.4.3 Human Resources

If you've ever wondered who keeps things running smoothly behind the scenes at a game studio, that's human resources (HR). They handle recruitment and onboarding, employment contracts, and compliance with labor laws. But it's not just paperwork – HR also helps shape studio culture, supports employee well-being with benefits like mental health resources, and may coordinate travel or logistics for team events or when the team hits the road for business. They might not be in the public eye, but without them, the studio wouldn't run nearly as smoothly.

2.4.4 Game Designers

Game designers are the masterminds behind the player experience. With their deep understanding of gameplay, they are responsible for the game's mechanics, systems, and rules that define how a game works and plays. This role comes with its own specializations, and each of them focuses on a different aspect of the game – some build engaging levels, while others balance combat, design puzzles, or weave interactive storylines. And without them? Well, there wouldn't be much of a game.

2.4.5 Programmers

Game programmers (also known as coders or engineers) are responsible for writing the code that makes a game function, from proprietary tools to game engines. Using programming languages like C++, C#, Python, or Java, they turn design concepts into functional systems, ensuring that art, sound, and gameplay elements all work together smoothly. Programming is one of the most technical aspects of game development, involving complex problem-solving, optimization, and close collaboration across disciplines.

2.4.6 Artists

Hey, that's you! Game artists bring the visuals of a game to life. Back in the early days, most of the art was actually done by programmers. But nowadays, game artists handle everything you see – from 2D and 3D characters and environments to animations, VFX, and UI. And within that, there's a whole bunch of specializations we'll go over in the next chapter.

2.4.7 Animators

Animators are artists too, no question – but their role deserves its own spotlight. They're the ones responsible for bringing characters, objects, and environments to life through movement. They create the animations for the player and non-playable characters (NPCs), such as walking, running, jumping, and interacting with objects.

2.4.8 Sound Designers

Sound designers create and implement the audio elements for a game – the footsteps, the rustling leaves, the tense music building up to a boss fight, you name it. They design sound effects for actions, environments, and characters, as well as the music and ambient sounds that set the mood. In addition, they also work on dialogue and voice-overs.

2.4.9 Writers

Game writers write the narrative and dialogue that drive a game's story. They develop the plot, create compelling characters, and write all the dialogue players will hear or read – from the lines in cinematic cutscenes to the tiniest details like pickup items or journal entries. But it's not just about words on a page. Game writers work closely with designers, artists, and voice actors to ensure the narrative aligns naturally with the gameplay and visual direction.

2.4.10 QA

The QA team is responsible for identifying and reporting any bugs and other game-related issues. They play through the game numerous times to check if it functions properly, meets the set quality standards, and provides a smooth experience for the players. QA testers play a very important role in ensuring the game functions well and is ready for release.

2.5 SENIORITY LEVELS

Like most roles in game development, game artists follow a clear career progression. Each step up the ladder represents more skills, more responsibility, and often leadership. *Figure 2.2* breaks down the art team by experience levels, though this can vary by studio. Your level, combined with your role, shapes the titles you'll often see: junior VFX artist, senior environment artist, principal character artist, lead animator, and so on.

The mid-level role (between junior and senior) usually doesn't carry a prefix, as it's considered the standard or "default" title.

You might also spot "associate" added to a title. What's that about? It typically indicates someone with more experience than a junior but not yet a full mid-level. For example, an associate character artist usually sits

Junior Artist

↓

Mid Artist

Senior Artist

Lead Artist   Principal Artist

Art Director

Creative
Director

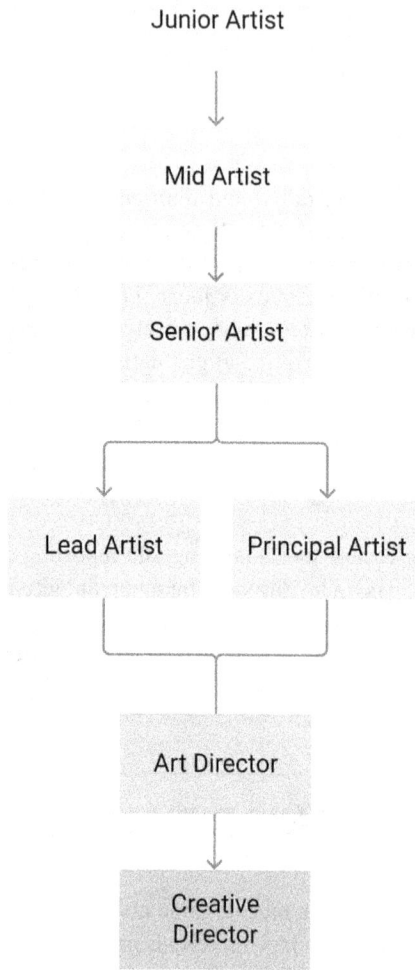

FIGURE 2.2 Common hierarchy of seniority levels.

between a junior and a mid-level character artist. Not every studio uses this title, but when they do, it helps clarify where someone fits on the experience ladder.

Larger teams can get even more specific. You might see "assistant," "associate," or "senior" paired with "lead" or "director" roles – like "associate lead" or "assistant art director" – to indicate seniority.

And to complicate things even further, some studios also use Roman numerals (I, II, and III) to mark sublevels within a role. For example, a senior artist I is less experienced than a senior artist III.

To keep things simple, we'll focus on the broad experience levels and skip the internal sublevels for now.

2.5.1 Junior

A junior artist is someone who has recently entered the industry, usually with 0–2 years of experience. At this stage, they are learning the ropes of the tools, workflows, and pipelines used in the studio. Junior artists work under the supervision of more experienced team members and focus on tasks that are less complex and manageable, allowing them to develop their skills and knowledge. As they gain more experience and expand their skills, they progressively take on more challenging and complex tasks, paving the way toward the mid-level position.

2.5.2 Mid-level

A mid-level artist, also known as a regular artist, is a professional with typically two to five years of experience working in the industry. As noted previously, titles at this level usually don't include a prefix – so unlike "junior" or "senior" concept artist, the role is typically listed simply as "concept artist." Mid-level artists have a solid understanding of their skills and the game development pipeline. At this stage, they can handle a broad range of tasks with minimal supervision and take on greater ownership of their work. This role is a stepping stone to the senior position, and they play an essential role in bridging the gap between junior and senior artists.

2.5.3 Senior

A senior artist, typically with 5+ years of experience, is highly skilled at both an artistic and a technical level. As experts in their field, they guide junior and mid-level artists to ensure that the quality of their work aligns with the studio's standards and the project's vision. They have strong communication and problem-solving skills, can collaborate closely with other departments, and can troubleshoot problems that arise during production. From this role, they can advance into a higher managerial position, such as lead artist, or transition into a senior specialist role as principal artist.

2.5.4 Principal

The principal artist is one of the most senior roles in the art department, typically with 8+ years of experience and a reputation for being exceptionally skilled. They're the go-to experts for pushing the boundaries of the game's visuals. Principal artists often handle the most challenging tasks, are great problem solvers, and collaborate closely with art directors, lead artists, and other senior roles to elevate the game's art quality. They also mentor artists across all levels, make critical creative decisions, and have a deep understanding of the industry tools, production pipelines, and optimization techniques.

2.5.5 Lead

The lead artist, typically with 5+ years of experience, oversees the art team to deliver high-quality assets that balance the project's creative vision with technical constraints. They delegate tasks based on team members' strengths, give feedback, and ensure work meets production goals in terms of quality and timeline. Lead artists collaborate closely with other leadership roles, departments, and outsourcing teams. They help establish the art pipeline and write clear documentation, often in collaboration with principal and senior artists. They provide the resources and mentorship their team needs to thrive, both during development and as they advance in their careers.

2.5.6 Art Director

The art director is responsible for setting the overall visual direction and art style of the game. This includes the look and feel of the game world, characters, environments, animations, VFX, UI, and other art assets. They work closely with all art teams to execute that vision in terms of visuals and make sure they meet production goals. They also work with departments other than art, including design, narrative, and technical teams, to ensure that the game's art aligns with the gameplay, story, and technical constraints.

This role is not only about artistic skill but also about strong leadership. Art directors inspire and guide the entire art department, providing direction, feedback, and mentorship. They're often hands-on, contributing to concepts, offering visual reference material, and helping keep production aligned with the project's vision and timeline.

2.5.7 Creative Director

Though both the creative director and the art director are senior roles, they focus on different parts of the game. The previously mentioned art director owns the game's visual side – the look, style, and feel of everything you see. The creative director, on the other hand, guides the overall creative vision – story, gameplay, art, and sound – making sure it all comes together.

They lead the broader creative team and work closely with producers and technical directors to keep the game's vision real and achievable within budgets and deadlines.

You might've heard of the game director, too. Their role overlaps with the creative director but leans more into gameplay mechanics and technical systems. Their job is to keep the game fun and running smoothly, while the creative director focuses on the overall creative direction.

2.6 ART TEAM STRUCTURE

Following the breakdown of seniority levels, it's important to understand how these roles actually fit within the art team's overall structure.

Usually, the art team is subdivided into specialized groups based on discipline, such as characters, environments, concepts, and VFX, among others.

But before we go further, here is a quick clarification: throughout this book, you'll see me use both "discipline" and "specialization." They're often used interchangeably to describe areas of expertise within game art.

That said, "specialization" can also go one level deeper. It's sometimes used to describe subspecialization: more focused roles within a discipline, for example, a character artist who focuses solely on facial rigging or hair, or an environment artist who's all about vegetation.

It's also worth noting that studio structures can vary significantly. How an art team is organized often depends on the studio's size, culture, and the types of projects they're working on. Still, there are a few common setups you'll see again and again:

2.6.1 Centralized Leadership

In small studios, art direction is often handled by one person – sometimes a dedicated art director, but just as often a lead artist – who oversees all art disciplines such as character, environment, and VFX. When a separate lead artist is present, they typically manage the day-to-day work and coordinating efforts between disciplines. There might also be one principal role above all disciplines – or multiple principals spread across the sub-teams, as shown in Figure 2.3. The disciplines shown in the figure (Character, Environment, VFX, UI, and Tech) are only examples; the actual number and type of disciplines may vary depending on the project's needs.

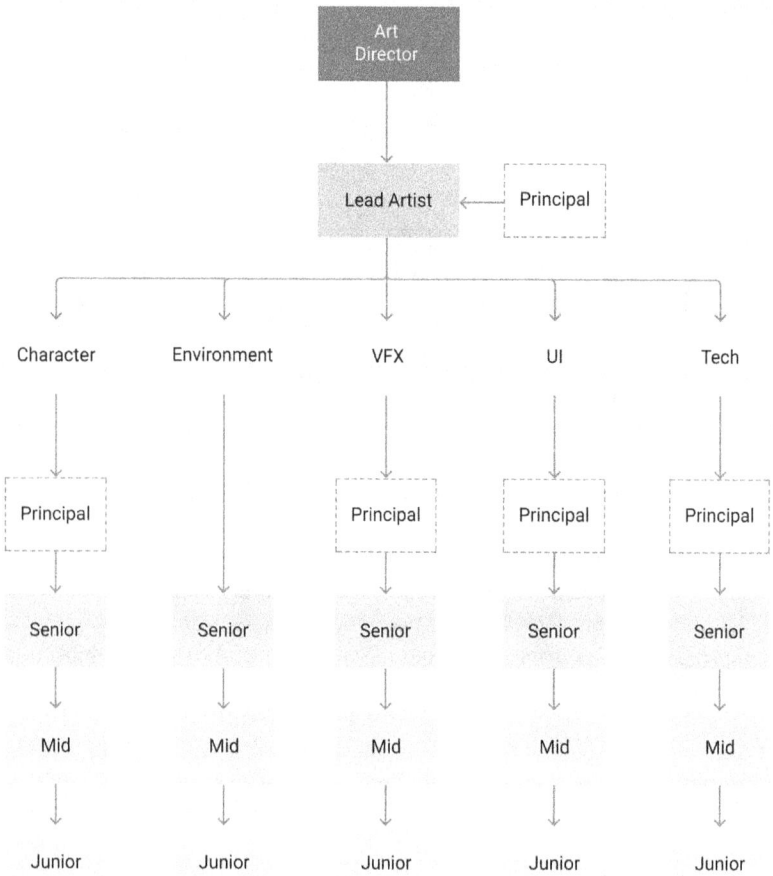

FIGURE 2.3   Centralized structure with one art director and a single lead artist managing all discipline-based teams.

2.6.2 Discipline-Specific Leadership

As studios grow in size, they tend to have more specialization (*Figure 2.4*). The art director still oversees everything, but there are multiple leads, each focused on a discipline like character, environment, and VFX. This allows leads to stay close to the work while maintaining clear ownership of their specialized discipline. Some teams might also have a principal position. This structure supports clearer workflows and coordination between disciplines.

2.6.3 Global Leadership

In large or global studios with complex, multilayered teams, you might find a global art director overseeing the art direction across multiple projects or

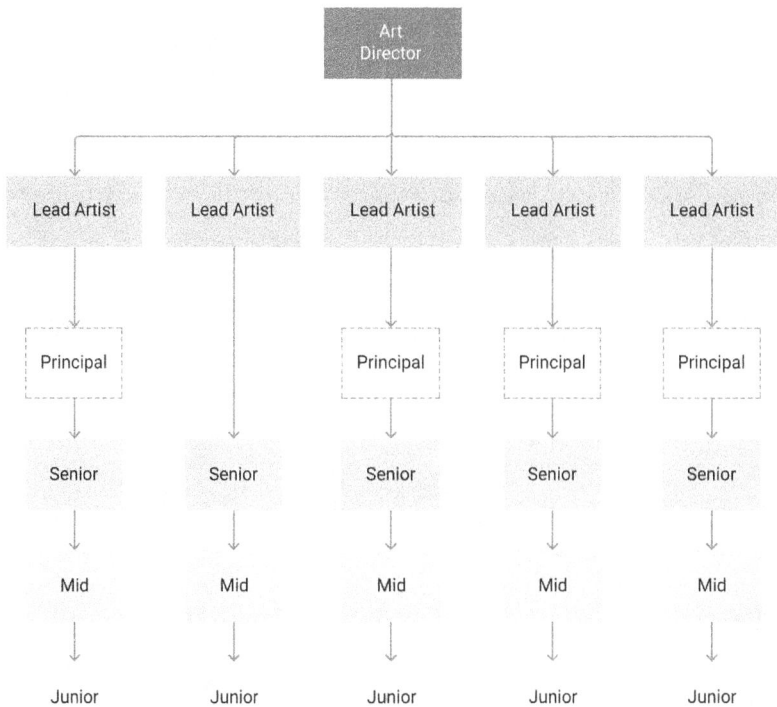

FIGURE 2.4   Discipline-specific structure with a single art director overseeing multiple lead artists, each managing their own discipline-based team.

studios simultaneously (Figure 2.5). Beneath them, it's common to have multiple art directors, each responsible for a specific project or a major area of a game, managing their own leads and teams semi-independently.

In these setups, artists often become highly specialized, with roles like vegetation artists within environment art or groom artists within character art, as covered earlier. With teams distributed across different locations, strong communication and well-defined pipelines are important for maintaining consistency.

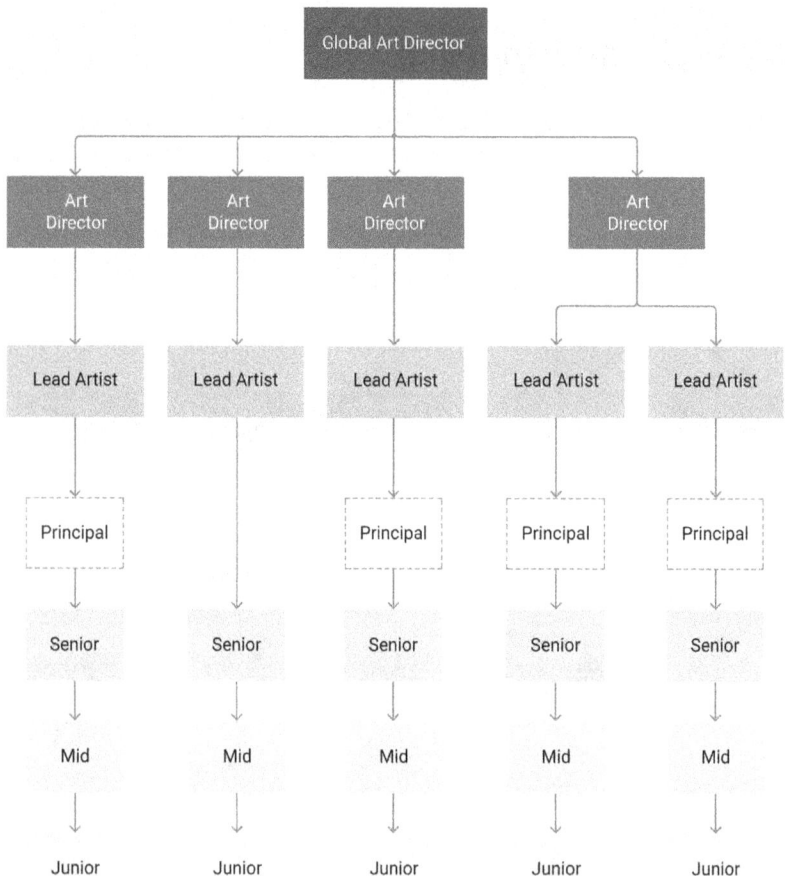

FIGURE 2.5 Global leadership structure with a global art director overseeing multiple art directors, each managing one or more lead artists who oversee their own discipline-based team.

2.7 THE HARSH REALITY OF GAME DEVELOPMENT

Let me be real with you: working in game development is not always glitz and glamour. Behind the scenes, developers often face challenges like overtime, project cancellations, studio closures, and layoffs – and that's only if you've managed to land a job in this insanely competitive industry to begin with.

I believe it's important to talk about these subjects to prepare you in the best way possible. The more prepared you are for the realities, the better you can set yourself up for success and manage your expectations.

2.7.1 Competitive Landscape and Demand

Breaking into the games industry? Yeah, it's tough. Tons of people are competing for each job, even at entry-level positions. Every year, waves of new graduates flood the job market, adding to an already crowded pool of talent. At major studios, it's not unusual to see hundreds of applicants for a single role. And with remote work becoming more common, the competition has gone global, making things even more intense.

2.7.2 Crunch Culture and Burnout

Crunch culture: you've probably heard of it. The intense periods of overtime, where developers push themselves to the limit, working long hours, sometimes for weeks or months, just to meet those critical deadlines.

Sure, it might seem like a quick way to ship a game on time, but at what cost? Crunch can take a hefty toll on your physical and mental health. The exhaustion, the stress, and the never-ending cycle – it will all eventually lead to burnout. When that happens, motivation and creativity begin to fade, and as a result, many talented people decide to leave the industry for good.

The good news? More and more companies are starting to realize the damage crunch can do. There's a growing movement toward creating healthier work environments, promoting flexible hours, and better planning to prevent these crunch periods from becoming the norm. It's not perfect, but change is on the horizon.

2.7.3 Project Cancellations

Project cancellations are more common than you'd think. A game can be shelved for all kinds of reasons: budget issues, market shifts, technical hurdles, or even a studio's change in direction. The unfortunate reality is that cancellations can happen at any point in the development process, even when you're near the finish line.

When a project is axed, it's not just a professional blow. It's personal. After months, sometimes years, of hard work, developers are left to watch their hard work never see the light of day. But it's not just the time invested that stings – it's the loss of passion and vision that gets sidelined.

For artists, this can be especially tough. Many times, cancelled projects remain locked down under strict non-disclosure agreements (NDAs), meaning you can't show the artwork you've made for the game to third parties (including your portfolio). This makes it especially difficult for some to prove their current skills and expertise to potential new employers if their portfolio is outdated.

2.7.4 Studio Closures and Layoffs

And in more severe cases, cancellations are followed by studio-wide layoffs or even shutdowns. Whether due to financial challenges, market conditions, cancelled projects, or the end of a production cycle, many talented individuals can find themselves suddenly out of work. The numbers don't lie – according to the Games Industry Layoffs Tracker,[2] more than 33,000 industry professionals have been laid off over the past three years, with around 14,600 layoffs in 2024 alone, as shown in Figure 2.6. Even developers with strong portfolios and solid resumes are having a hard time finding work.

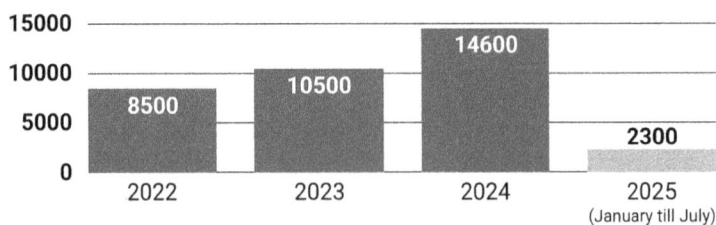

FIGURE 2.6   Game industry layoffs from 2022 to mid-2025. Based on data from the Games Industry Layoffs Tracker, used with permission.

Source: https://publish.obsidian.md/vg-layoffs/Archive/2025.

At the time of writing in mid-2025, the job market remains tough. Approximately 2,300 layoffs had already been reported in the first half of the year. While that's lower than in previous years, the total may still rise as more data becomes available.

2.7.5 Why It's Still a Rewarding Career

It can feel overwhelming at first, and you might even be asking yourself, "Why would anyone choose a career in game development?" And to be honest, that's a valid question. But for those who stick with it, the payoff can be incredibly rewarding. You get to watch as players from around the world get lost in the worlds you helped build, reacting to every detail you and your team meticulously crafted. There's something deeply satisfying in knowing that your work is fueling someone else's experience.

And if that's not enough, depending on where you land, there could be opportunities for you to travel the world – attending game conferences or collaborating with international teams – adding another layer of adventure to your career.

But hey, if you're feeling the weight of it all, I get it. Just remember, we're only scratching the surface here. There's much more to come in this book, and we're not even halfway through yet. If you're genuinely passionate about game development, nothing is holding you back.

> *"Nothing beats the high of a release day YouTube playthrough where you hear the words, 'This game looks stunning.'"*
>
> – Shona Markusen

NOTES

1 Plato, Republic 2.377a–b, trans. Paul Shorey (Perseus Digital Library, https://perseus.tufts.edu), CC BY-SA 3.0 US.
2 Games Industry Layoffs Tracker, "Archive/2025," https://publish. obsidian.md/vg-layoffs/Archive/2025.

Specializations

3

At some point in your career, you'll face a big question: should you specialize in one area or go the generalist route? I hear this question all the time – and to be honest, there's no right or wrong answer.

Most students start as generalists, learning a bit of everything through their course curricula. I recommend doing the same and dabbling a bit in each. Then, as you grow and explore, you'll likely find yourself naturally drawn to something specific, like character art, environments, or animation.

Specializing sharpens your skills, helps you stand out, and increases your chances of landing a job. But don't choose based only on job trends or salary potential. Knowing the market is smart, but building a career around something you don't enjoy? That's a quick road to burnout.

You want this to be sustainable. Something you can grow with over time, not something that drains you.

Here's the good news: choosing a specialization isn't a life sentence. Many skills transfer across roles, and with enough discipline, switching paths later is completely doable.

So what are your options? Game art includes many specializations and even more subspecializations – far too many to cover here. To keep things focused, this chapter highlights the most common ones, each featuring an interview with a professional working in that field.

3.1 CONCEPT ARTIST

Before production even kicks off, concept artists are the ones designing characters, environments, creatures, and props and setting the mood for the entire game. They tackle visual challenges early on, laying the groundwork for everything that comes after.

DOI: 10.1201/9781003492320-3

Their job is about more than just drawing; it's about solving problems, establishing the game's aesthetic, and creating a visual language that everyone on the team can follow.

INTERVIEW WITH DAMIAN AUDINO, FREELANCE CONCEPT ARTIST

Q: Tell us a bit about yourself.
A: My name is Damian Audino, I've been a Senior Concept Artist for about 8 years now, and have worked with companies like Netherrealm, Bethesda, Rocksteady, Blizzard, amongst many others!

Q: What inspired you to pursue this career?
A: I was working in a warehouse and was drawing during my lunch break. One of the truck drivers came over and told me it was pretty good and maybe I should think about pursuing that, instead of working there! So it wasn't inspiration but more the fact that drawing has always been a part of me, and someone else just let me know I could actually do something with it. So I thank him for that!

Q: How did you get your first job as a Concept Artist?
A: I uploaded my work on ArtStation and made a portfolio. I can't remember my very first paid job honestly, but I got a lot of work through reaching the front page on there, but this was years ago. I'm not sure how often that would happen now as there are so many pieces going up everyday.

Q: What tools do you use?
A: Photoshop, 3D Coat, Blender, ZBrush.

Q: What's your favourite part of the job?
A: Coming up with ideas on how things work, the actual concepting and ideation stage of things.

Q: What's your least favourite?
A: Over-rendering, being rushed, and contradicting feedback.

Q: What are the most valuable skills?
A: Draftsmanship and a curiosity in the world.

Q: What are some useful but optional skills?
A: Soft skills like being able to communicate effectively, time management for yourself or team, being adaptable, taking feedback well, and implementing it correctly. Many of these sorts of "life" skills aren't only nice to have – they're essential for working in a studio environment and being someone others enjoy working with. You could be the best artist in the world, but if no one likes your attitude, you'll find it hard to interview and hard to retain a job in a studio, at least.

Q: How would you describe your typical working day?

A: Wake up early because my son is up at 5:30 a.m. most mornings! Coffee, get him ready for school, do the drop off, then sit down and start working, whether that's checking emails or feedback from the previous day, or continuing where I left off the day before. Then I usually work out at lunchtime, then go back to the desk until my son comes home. Cook dinner, get him ready for bed, then back on the computer to either keep working a little or maybe do some personal stuff. Also, if I have a game I'm playing, I'll fit a bit of that in as well somewhere (not much time anymore though).

Q: What's a common misconception about Concept Artists?

A: I have had people think it's like animation, but most have no idea how anything 3D actually works. When I explain a program like Blender, sometimes it's like I'm talking an alien language.

Q: What advice would you give to newcomers?

A: Become good at drawing, understand how to construct anything with a pen and paper, understand 3D forms on a 2D page, and you will be good to go. For most things, even sculpting and painting are easier once you know how to draw properly. Don't rely on photos or AI to do the work for you.

3.2 2D ARTIST

2D artists specialize in designing and producing two-dimensional assets, from backgrounds and icons to splash screens, promotional illustrations, hand-painted textures, pixel art, and fully animated sprites.

In 2D games, their work often defines the visual style, where their illustrations and animations can become central to the player's experience.

INTERVIEW WITH OLIVER ELM, SENIOR 2D ARTIST (AND NARRATIVE DESIGNER)

Q: Tell us a bit about yourself.

A: I'm Oliver Elm, 2D Artist and Narrative Designer from Sweden. Been in the games industry since 2014, where I've worked primarily on the *Steamworld* game series. Outside of games, I write and illustrate children's books and work on personal indie game projects.

Q: What inspired you to pursue this career?

A: I grew up watching lots of cartoons and reading lots of comics. This led to a love of drawing, and I wanted to be an artist for as long as can remember. Once I realized you could work in video games and be an artist and have "a real job" at the same time, I knew what I had to become. I ended up in 2D art because that's the type of art I enjoy doing the most.

Q: How did you get your first job as a 2D Artist?

A: My education (The Game Assembly) ended with an internship. I made a 2D-heavy portfolio and got an internship as a 2D artist at a studio that made 2D games. After my internship, I was hired at that studio.

Q: What tools do you use?

A: Adobe Photoshop, Adobe Illustrator, Adobe After Effects.

Q: What's your favourite part of the job?

A: Getting to draw fun and interesting things for a living, and seeing it all come together in a game.

Q: What's your least favourite?

A: Drawn out concept stages where you draw different versions of the same thing again and again, until decision makers finally become happy.

Q: What are the most valuable skills?

A: Besides drawing and painting, the ability to see the whole game, not just the piece you're working on. If you understand where your drawing fits and how it connects to other parts of the game, you'll make something that will fit in perfectly.

Q: What are some useful but optional skills?

A: A basic understanding of 3D modelling can help you a lot. Making a simple 3D model and then painting on top of it can save you a lot of time.

Q: How would you describe your typical working day?

A: Draw a quick concept for an asset, send it to the Art Director for approval, then spend the rest of the day drawing and painting the asset in the game's final art style. Or start working right away based on a concept somebody else has done.

Q: What's a common misconception about 2D Artists?

A: That it's enough to be amazing at drawing or painting to be a good 2D game artist. You need to put in the effort to learn how the technical aspect of the art pipeline works too. A little bit of tech knowledge can bring you a long way and make your teammates really appreciate you.

Q: What advice would you give to newcomers?

A: Study the basics of art. Anatomy, perspective, light, etc. They will help you in everything you do, even in stylized video game graphics.

3.3 CHARACTER ARTIST

Character artists are responsible for creating the 3D models of characters that players see and interact with in the game, from the player and story characters to enemies, creatures, and other NPCs. This role blends artistic creativity with technical skill, as character artists sculpt detailed characters and ensure models are optimized for animation and gameplay. They need a strong grasp of anatomy and clothing design, along with storytelling details that make each character unique and memorable.

INTERVIEW WITH JUAN NOVELLETTO, SENIOR CHARACTER ARTIST

Q: Would you mind telling us a bit about yourself?

A: I'm Juan Novelletto, currently working as a Senior Character and Creature Artist. With 9+ years of experience in the industry, I've had the pleasure of working on some of the biggest video game titles, including *Doom: The Dark Ages*, *Mortal Kombat 11*, *Mortal Kombat 1* (2023), *Injustice 2*, *Gotham Knights*, and *Total War: Warhammer III*. Not only do I specialize in character art for video games, but I'm also a digital sculptor for collectibles. I've had the honor of working with renowned companies such as XM Studios, Witchsong, Mindwork Games, Baobab Miniatures, and Heramodels.

Q: What inspired you to pursue this career?

A: I've always been passionate about drawing, a passion that began in childhood and was inspired by my parents, both artists – my mother a sculptor and my father a painter. Growing up, our house was filled with art books that fueled my creativity. What I loved most about drawing, more than anything, was creating characters. After years of working as a web developer, I discovered the ZBrush forum and Wacom tablets – it was love at first sight. Something clicked in my mind, and I decided to learn as much as I could, as quickly as possible. Back then, accessing information wasn't as easy as it is now, but I managed to teach myself. A few years later, I built a concept art portfolio, which opened the door to my first opportunities and launched my career. Once I was working in the AAA industry and saw the incredible work of character artists, I knew that was what I wanted to become.

Q: How did you get your first job as a Character Artist?

A: As I mentioned before, while I was already working in the industry as a concept artist, I started getting more and more interested in character art. At that time, I was working at NXA Studios (now Collider Craftworks), an outsourcing studio in Argentina that specializes in character work. We were developing characters for *Mortal Kombat 11*, and I was in charge of designing concepts for the gear system. Even though I appreciated the work, I wasn't fully satisfied with that role, and seeing what the character artists were doing made me realize it aligned much more with what I wanted to do. So I talked to my art director and asked if they could assign me a character, giving me a bit more time to learn what I needed. That's how I created my very first character in production.

Q: What tools do you use?

A: Nothing too crazy, but if I had to list them: ZBrush for high poly sculpting, Marvelous Designer for cloth simulation, Maya for retopology and UVs, and Substance Painter for texturing. Throughout my career, I've worked on projects using Unity, Unreal, and also proprietary engines. I also love experimenting with new tools whenever I can.

Q: What's your favourite part of the role?

A: Definitely the blocking phase. That's where the character is truly defined. If something fails there, everything will likely fall apart later on. Working on proportions, overall shapes, and silhouette – in my opinion, that's the most important part of creating a character for games. The focus should be on how clearly the character reads. In a video game, our character isn't static; they exist in a world with dynamic lighting, movement, and other characters. Often, they'll be seen in motion most of the time. In the blocking phase, we shape all of that, and it's also where we need to fully understand the visual language of the project we're working on. My second favorite stage is texturing, because just like blocking, it helps to reinforce the readability of the character. Plus, it's a great moment to add a lot of detail without going back into ZBrush.

Q: What's your least favourite part of the role?

A: Honestly, I really enjoy every part of the process. But if I had to pick one, I'd say that in projects that require an extremely high level of detail, that stage can sometimes feel a bit repetitive or boring. But I'm not complaining – I love what I do!

Q: What are the most valuable skills for your role?

A: It depends on many factors and on each project, but I'd say being able to interpret a concept well is a very valuable skill, especially being able to solve everything that's not explicitly defined. Having good communication with other departments, like animation and FX, is also key to avoid issues down the line. And above all, understanding that you're part of something bigger, so being a good teammate is fundamental.

Q: What are some useful but optional skills?

A: If we're talking strictly professional aspects, and based on my own experience, I'd say it's very valuable to be someone who's always looking for solutions to potential problems. Being able to give feedback to other artists and mentor junior teammates is also a big plus. Managing outsourcing teams is a strong skill to have as well, along with being able to clearly communicate the vision of the lead and art director.

Q: How would you describe your typical working day?

A: It depends on which stage of a character I'm working on, but generally, there's always some meeting during the day where we discuss the project in general or give feedback to the team. As for my tasks, I basically focus on advancing a character and communicating with other departments if I have any questions or potential issues.

Q: What's a common misconception about Character Artists?

A: If it's someone outside the industry, I'd say it's not very clear what being a character artist means. In general, in the AAA industry, roles tend to be very specialized, and if this isn't known, people might think a character artist is perhaps a generalist 3D artist who even does animation.

Q: What advice would you give to newcomers?

A: Being very specific, it's a long journey that requires discipline and, therefore, time dedication. Keep this in mind, and understand that things take time, so try to manage anxiety. Practically speaking, build a portfolio with two or three high-quality pieces, showcasing the entire workflow – not just beauty renders, but also wireframes, UVs, texture sets, etc. Set small goals and achieve them, always stay in practice, sketch a lot, study anatomy, color theory, etc. The fundamentals are just that, fundamental. And above all, enjoy the journey!

3.4 ENVIRONMENT ARTIST

Environment artists design and build the game's surroundings – from lush forests and urban streets to alien landscapes and ancient ruins. They use modeling, texturing, and lighting to create immersive, believable spaces that enhance atmosphere, support gameplay, and reinforce the narrative.

Their work often involves modularity, creating reusable assets like architectural building blocks or rock formations that can be used from multiple angles and across different locations. This approach ensures efficiency while maintaining visual consistency.

Through all of this, environment artists help define the game's visual language and transform virtual spaces into rich, explorable worlds that draw players in.

INTERVIEW WITH JULIAN ELWOOD, SENIOR ENVIRONMENT ARTIST AT NAUGHTY DOG

Q: Tell us a bit about yourself.

A: Hi, I'm Julian Elwood from Denver, Colorado, and I'm a Senior Environment Artist at Naughty Dog! I moved to LA in 2015, aiming for art school, but got a rejection letter on the day I arrived. Searching online that day, I found Gnomon just a few blocks away, enrolled, and graduated in 2018. I'm so grateful things turned out this way, and I always recommend students not to grasp too tightly to a particular school or dream job; you never know where your path will lead.

After graduation, I landed my first job through The Rookies website at NetherRealm Studios, working on *Mortal Kombat 11*. I moved to Chicago for that contract and shipped my first game there. After that, I took Naughty Dog's art test and was hired for a three-month contract at the very end of *The Last of Us Part II* development, which turned into a full-time role, and I've been there since!

Q: What inspired you to pursue this career?

A: I was inspired by a behind-the-scenes DVD that came with *God of War II* on PS2. Showing how games are made is crucial to drawing in new developers, and I wish more studios did that! Initially, I wanted to pursue concept art, which is a common starting point since many don't know about other specializations. I certainly didn't. But what drew me to environment art specifically? I think I was always more inclined toward the more technical side of 3D art, and have always had an interest in game design and player psychology. Environment art blends technical, artistic, and design skills, making it a unique and design-adjacent specialization.

Q: How did you get your first job as an Environment Artist?

A: After graduating, I submitted a portfolio to "The Rookies" site, which is a contest for art students. Although I didn't win, I got contacted by the recruiter from NetherRealm after they saw my post there!

Q: What tools do you use?

A: Maya is my 3D modeling tool. Recently, I've been exploring Houdini more. While I don't think most environment art requires Houdini, its usage and procedural modeling techniques will only increase in the future, I believe. For texturing, I use Substance Designer and Substance Painter. I also sketch on paper because I find environment design easier to plan in 2D.

Q: What's your favourite part of the job?

A: My favorite part is how integrated you are into the experiential side of the development process while still being creative. Environments are foundational to gameplay, though less flashy than characters or concept art. I like to think that environment artists are like the bassists in a band – essential but less noticed. What really excites me about environments is thinking deeply about player experience and gameplay.

Q: What's your least favourite?

A: -

Q: What are the most valuable skills?

A: Difficult to pick just one, but the best is the ability to focus on the most useful tasks. Environment artists juggle many tools and systems that are whole professions in their own right. Diving too deep wastes time on details players won't see or that get optimized out. It's about maximizing quality for the time invested. I sometimes get caught in perfecting Substance designs or node-based systems, but have learned to aim for "good enough" and get assets into the game engine quickly. Think of it like an equation: time invested equals resolution gained, up to a point. Knowing when to stop is a skill in itself.

Q: What are some useful but optional skills?

A: Communication skills are mandatory. If no one wants to work with you, skills don't matter. Especially post-pandemic, it's easy to disappear if you only attend mandatory meetings. Also, being able to discuss gameplay and design clearly is key. Games are experiential, so describing what an experience feels like before it exists is a unique challenge. I recommend everyone have a "red wine" game: a game you immerse yourself in fully, and write about what stood out and why. Bring those ideas into an articulated space, rather than something you passively feel while you're playing.

Q: How would you describe your typical working day?

A: Environment artists have it pretty good. We're given a task and often left weeks to complete it with few meetings interrupting. The tasks vary by project phase. I usually start my day with coffee, then play through the level I'm working on to identify improvements and find the lowest-hanging fruit that will increase quality the fastest. Then I'll work through that checklist until a check-in or feedback from leads or artists around me. Rinse and repeat until we ship!

Q: What's a common misconception about Environment Artists?

A: Students sometimes ask if I play games at work since I have a PlayStation at my desk. There's much less playing than they think. Games take an immense amount of time to finish, and unless in playtest, most time is spent making art. Another misconception is that we build all assets from scratch. Studio work is very collaborative. Your job is to build environments using any available resources, and being familiar with your team's assets well enough to combine and save time is an important skill.

Q: What advice would you give to newcomers?

A: Scope down your personal work. You can get hired on a single high-quality prop, and if you provide well-thought-out breakdowns of your process alongside it. If I see an incredible prop on a portfolio that communicates a high level of artistic intuition and execution, I can easily assume that person can repeat that process several hundred times for a full environment. What's popular on ArtStation right now are vast environments, and while these are cool, they can be very overwhelming for new artists to tackle. So don't think the scale of your composition equates to value in your portfolio. It's far more frequent that I see a large environment look good at one camera angle, but the second you zoom in, or move the camera, the quality disappears. I'd rather see an environment artist make one well-executed photoreal building than an entire poorly executed city.

3.5 PROP ARTIST

Prop artists create the interactive and decorative objects that populate a game world, from detailed set pieces and artifacts to everyday items like books, crates, or lamps. We often take objects for granted in a game, but without them, the world would feel incomplete.

They're reusable across locations and tailored to the game's unique art style. Every detail – from scale and material to wear and tear – tells a story about the world they belong to. Props are what make the world feel authentic, immersive, and lived-in.

INTERVIEW WITH QUINN BOGAERTS, 3D PROP ARTIST

Q: Tell us a bit about yourself.

A: My name is Quinn Bogaerts, I'm a Prop Artist with a preference for hard surface and over three years of experience in the industry. I've worked on projects such as *Star Wars Outlaws*, Ubisoft's *XDefiant*, and more. When I'm not making props, I'll either be playing my accordion or having a beer at the local pub.

Q: What inspired you to pursue this career?

A: After initially pursuing a career in concept art, I quickly realized I preferred bringing concepts to life and building on them rather than creating them and only going up to a certain point. I've always been fascinated by 3D detail on toys and figurines, and spending my day creating those details is something I can't get enough of.

Q: How did you get your first job as a Prop Artist?

A: I spontaneously applied for an internship at Ubisoft Annecy, and got offered a contract when my internship ended. I had some short previous experience illustrating and concepting for 3D animation.

Q: What tools do you use?

A: I use Blender and ZBrush to model, Marmoset and Substance Painter to bake, Substance Painter to texture, and Blender to render. I try to do as much as possible in Blender, though. Depending on the production workflow, I might spend a lot of time in the game engine.

Q: What's your favourite part of the job?

A: Rendering the final result. Even if a prop for production doesn't need any renders, I'll sneak a couple in if I'm happy with what I made. I usually do these in Blender using Cycles.

Q: What's your least favourite?

A: Depending on the workflow production is using, changing a small detail after finishing a prop can require quite a big rework. Prop production is kind of split up into a couple of steps. If the change requires going back to step one, having to also redo a lot of the work in the following steps is not something I particularly enjoy. Having to do extra optimizing passes at the end of a project can be quite painful too.

Q: What are the most valuable skills?

A: I think if looking at a skill specific to prop art, I would say an eye for detail. Most of the work that goes into props will go unnoticed by most players, but they will notice when the detail is not there. Props are a big part of selling the believability of the game world. Knowing how to interpret concepts and references plays heavily into this too. To me, a good prop is not necessarily identical to a concept; rather, it needs to properly convey the ideas portrayed in the concept to the player in a believable way.

Q: What are some useful but optional skills?

A: As a Prop Artist, you are often making props that will go through other teams at some point (Level Art, Game Design, Level Design, Art Direction, . . .). The more the Prop Artist knows about other roles, the better they can anticipate any problems or requirements, and ensure a smooth process with good communication and minimal rework. Even though making props can often be a solitary process, good soft skills are required.

Q: How would you describe your typical working day?

A: Usually, I always have a prop to work on, and most of my time is spent going through that process: modeling, unwrapping, texturing, maybe even making a high poly and baking. This can take up to multiple weeks. This process is broken up by regularly checking in on the people who will use the prop once it is done, to be sure the result will be able to do what is needed. I usually scroll through ArtStation in the morning, and will often get up to see what my colleagues are working on at some point during the day.

Q: What's a common misconception about Prop Artists?

A: A Prop Artist needs a good artistic and technical perspective on what they are doing. It is not one or the other. A common misconception I've heard in AAA is that a prop artist does not texture their own props, but that this would be the job of a Material/Texture Artist. Texturing can be the most time-intensive part of the prop creation process.

Q: What advice would you give to newcomers?

A: I think it's best to only pursue a career in props if it is something you are passionate about. Also, as with all career paths led by passion, be wary of companies trying to exploit that.

3.6 HARD-SURFACE ARTIST

Hard-surface artists focus on mechanical and manufactured assets: vehicles, weapons, robots, armor, (sci-fi) architecture, and any object requiring precision and sharp edges. They use techniques like subdivision modeling, Boolean operations, and careful UV mapping to create clean, crisp geometry.

This role blends creativity with technical problem-solving. Every curve, joint, and edge must serve both form and function, making hard-surface modeling as much about logic and problem-solving as it is about style.

INTERVIEW WITH DYLAN MELLOTT, SENIOR 3D HARD-SURFACE ARTIST

Q: Tell us a bit about yourself.
A: My name is Dylan Mellott, I'm a Senior 3D Hard-Surface Artist with ten years of experience working professionally in games. I've worked on both small and large teams in AAA, as well as at indie studios. I've been lucky to work on several *Battlefield* titles, as well as many *Destiny 2* expansions and seasons. Outside of work, I like to strength train, cycle on my road bike, work on personal projects, play and run tabletop *Cyberpunk* and *DnD5e* campaigns, socialize with my friends, and enjoy some peaceful time at home with my partner and our three cats.

Q: What inspired you to pursue this career?
A: I've loved games since I was five, but never imagined art would be the path. I've always been fascinated by sci-fi, robots, and mechas. When I went to art school, I found Polycount and other forums where artists were creating exactly these things. I realized I could learn from these communities to start creating them myself.

Q: How did you get your first job as a Hard-Surface Artist?
A: It was the result of several overlapping things:

- Community engagement – I was actively participating in online art circles and forums like Polycount and Ten Thousand Hours, not just posting but also engaging with other artists' work.
- Consistent practice – I was constantly working on my portfolio after my office day job, treating building my skills and portfolio basically like a second job.
- Iterative improvement – Taking feedback seriously, implementing it, and refining my projects until they were truly portfolio-ready.
- Relationship building – Most importantly, I was building a network of peers and friends who later became my pathway into the industry. Events like game dev mixers and GDC were huge for this.

Q: What tools do you use?
A: Blender and Plasticity are my main modeling tools. Plasticity speeds up shape-building significantly. I also use Marmoset Toolbag 5, Substance Painter, ZBrush, Photoshop, and PureRef.

Q: What's your favourite part of the job?

A: This is tough because there are several aspects I love. I grew up playing games and still do, so I'm always tuned into the latest coming out of the industry. Being able to do this for a living feels incredibly lucky – I'm still a fan myself. There's something surreal about seeing your work pop up in YouTube videos and watching people get genuinely excited about it. This career has also given me some of my best friends while opening my perspective to many new things.

Q: What's your least favourite?

A: The word that comes to mind is "pressure." There's a lingering sense of urgency that never goes away, and the learning never stops. But with healthy habits, it's manageable.

Q: What are the most valuable skills?

A: Without a doubt:

- Dependability
- Adaptability
- Communication
- Kindness
- Empathy
- Honesty

See how I haven't mentioned any art-specific skills yet? It's because I firmly believe that if you uphold and embody these, the rest will fall into place.

Now, for art-specific skills:

- Critical Thinking – You must be able to put yourself in the shoes of a player. Your design choices should serve the player experience.
- Functionality – This isn't a catch-all rule, but the key is asking yourself if there are ways to make your art more believable. Look for evidence in the real world and bend it slightly to fit your needs.

Q: What are some useful but optional skills?

A: The longer I've worked, the more powerful it is to know some code or shader setup. You can create eye-catching 3D art, but knowing how to apply cool effects really makes the work stand out. It broadens your skillset, so it's a win-win.

Q: How would you describe your typical working day?

A: I start by checking emails and urgent items. Then continue whatever asset is tasked, taking it through the pipeline: blockout, mesh test, high/low poly modeling, UV, bake, texture, and final polish.

Some days have art reviews or playtests, so I prepare by ensuring work is presentable for feedback. I also gather references, collaborate with other artists, and ensure assets meet tech requirements.

The variety keeps things interesting. No two days are alike.

Q: What's a common misconception about Hard-Surface Artists?
A: Weapons are characters. They need the same degree of thought and personality that any top-tier video game character would have. Hard-surface work is highly specialized, with many technical pitfalls like buckled normals, broken lighting, edge seams, UV stretching, etc., that can take years to fully understand.

Q: What advice would you give to newcomers?
A: It's absolutely possible. I never imagined I could make 3D weapons for a living – but here I am, and you can get here too.

Build a focused, high-quality portfolio that demonstrates quality over quantity. Study real-world references: how things are built, how they wear, how materials behave. This makes your work feel authentic.

Engage with the art community, give feedback, ask questions, and build relationships.

Be open to critique. Your first models won't be perfect, and that's OK. Stay persistent. Most importantly, train your artistic eye – software can be taught, but artistic judgement takes time and practice.

3.7 MATERIAL ARTIST

Material artists focus on creating surfaces – such as wood, metal, fabric, or stone – that define how objects look and feel. They create materials with texture maps and shaders, carefully controlling properties such as color, roughness, and reflectivity. From a rusty door to a muddy trail, their work adds depth and believability to every surface in the game world.

INTERVIEW WITH ETIENNE BEDNARZ, SENIOR MATERIAL SPECIALIST/ENVIRONMENT ARTIST

Q: Tell us a bit about yourself.
A: Hey there! My name is Etienne Bednarz, I'm a Senior Material Specialist/Environment Artist at EA Motive with over 8 years of

game-industry experience (time flies). During my career, I had the privilege to work on several titles such as: *The Crew: Motorfest*, *Star Wars Outlaws*, *Avatar: Frontiers of Pandora*, and recently, the next *Battlefield* entry. Some of my hobbies include photography, urbex, cinema, traveling, and reading.

Q: What inspired you to pursue this career?

A: It came to me when I started making Half-Life 2 mods or Counter-Strike maps. I wanted to create new content, not to be restricted to what was in the game. Ultimately, it's creating new materials that stuck with me the most. Creating materials was one of the funniest parts to me.

Q: How did you get your first job as a Material Artist?

A: After getting my degree in Real-Time 3DCG at Haute École Albert Jacquard, I applied to several studios, one of which was Ivory-Tower (a Ubisoft Studio). After some interviews and a small art test, I got an offer that I accepted, but I'd like to mention that at that time, my portfolio was already mostly focused on material art.

Q: What tools do you use?

A: My main software is Substance Designer, as I love its very procedural approach and versatility. I also use Marmoset Toolbag for baking purposes, rendering, and more rarely ZBrush when I need sculpting.

Q: What's your favourite part of the job?

A: Lately, my favorite part is doing what we could call Material "Tech" Art Research and Development. I love working with Tech Artists and Render Programmers to find new solutions to problems or advance the quality of our render.

Q: What's your least favourite?

A: Redundancy. Doing only materials all day, every day for a long time can be quite straining.

Q: What are the most valuable skills?

A: The two most valuable skills, in my opinion, would be: understanding the physics and interactions between light and matter (more so than just knowing basic PBR guidelines), and knowing your metrics. These two will ensure your materials are always "grounded in reality" thanks to correct data (you can use that for stylized art also). More generically, you'll also need strong observation skills, just like in most image-related art.

Q: What are some useful but optional skills?
A: I think an interest in shaders is a huge plus, and so is an interest in the graphics rendering pipeline. It can be a huge help for optimization inside a shader to know how things work internally.

Q: How would you describe your typical working day?
A: My typical day of working would be as such:

* Prepare some tea!
* Check my to-do's and my priorities (if I have nothing, I'll sync up with my lead).
* Gather references corresponding to my task at hand (if you don't already have some), but also gather context about how/where it'll be used.
* Start working on my materials. I always start with only Height, Normal, and AO to get the surface of my materials right, and work on Color and Roughness only at a later stage.
* Once I'm happy with it, I export my material to test it in-engine and in-context: Now it's going to be back and forth between the engine and Substance Designer, where I'll tweak/polish/refine my materials and re-export to view my changes in engine.
* I then submit my work and have reviews/feedback with whoever is concerned about my task, be it some other Environment Artist, my Lead, or Art Director.
* Iterate following feedback if needed, otherwise you're done!
* Rinse and repeat!

Q: What's a common misconception about Material Artists?
A: It's a more technical job than most people think. You have to have a strong "solution-oriented" mind to create procedural materials efficiently.

Q: What advice would you give to newcomers?
A: As mentioned before, my first one would be to get a strong grasp of how light interacts with matter in the real world, as that'll help you understand PBR and go further. Following tutorials is perfectly fine; it'll help you get familiar with the tools/pipeline, but try not to post those tutorial pieces in your portfolio. Instead, use what you've learned to create your own original work. Always gather references, and always test your materials in different lighting conditions. Finally, don't shy away from asking for feedback online. There are plenty of communities ready to help you.

3.8 LIGHTING ARTIST

Lighting artists set the mood, atmosphere, and visual clarity of a game through the use of light. They place and adjust light sources to enhance environments, guide the player's attention, and support the storytelling. By controlling factors like intensity, color, shadows, and contrast, lighting artists help create immersive, believable worlds that feel alive, atmospheric, and dynamic.

INTERVIEW WITH GEOFFROY CALIS, SENIOR LIGHTING ARTIST AT REMEDY ENTERTAINMENT

Q: **Tell us a bit about yourself.**
A: My name is Geoffroy Calis, and I'm working as Lead Lighting Artist on *Control 2* at Remedy Entertainment. With over 12 years of experience, I have worked on multiple projects such as *Alan Wake 2*, *Battlefield 2042*, *Battlefield V*, *The Division*, and *Rainbow Six Siege*. With the opportunity to work on multiple game engines like Northlight, Frostbite, Snowdrop, Unreal Engine, and Anvil. In my spare time, I enjoy taking pictures of architecture and landscapes when traveling around the world, or of my two cats when staying home.

Q: **What inspired you to pursue this career?**
A: The thrill of pushing creativity and finding new challenges for each new project I worked on. Sometimes it's about the game itself, sometimes the tech used behind it, and other times the teams I worked with. Each project and company can give a different experience, and it's always exciting to take the steps to discover it.

Q: **How did you get your first job as a Lighting Artist?**
A: I started as a Level/Environment Artist at Kt Racing (then Kylotonn) in Paris after an internship, continuing on their early racing games. We were a small, multitasking team. Alongside modeling, texturing, and level art, I handled lighting and helped set up our first PBR workflow. Information was difficult to come by back then, and mostly present in forums.

At the time, Lighting Artist roles existed mainly at large studios with big teams, so their workflows were hard to access or fully understand.

My first real step into lighting came at Massive in Malmö. I began as a Level Artist on *The Division*, but my leads noticed my interest early on and offered me a transition. The lighting team was small, and with support from my colleagues, I quickly developed a strong foundation for what became my career.

Q: What tools do you use?
A: It depends on the engine, but many tools are similar across them. We use various features to create different light types, volumes for fog, post-process effects, reflections, and global illumination.
    We also rely on visualizers for performance checks, optimization, and exposure or post-process calibration.
    For software, DaVinci Resolve is a must for my color grading workflow. I often use Photoshop to tweak emissive maps or HDRi skies. I also use 3D software for modeling tweaks or more complex workflows, especially with Houdini.

Q: What's your favourite part of the job?
A: That's a hard choice . . . But I may choose the moment when my colleagues from other disciplines are sending some love comments to our team when we are doing the first pass of lighting. Despite still being a rough visual, everyone can finally see the full potential and start to bring more ideas along with feedback, and that will always make me smile.

Q: What's your least favourite?
A: As we are at the end of the production line, the lighting team is also very often forgotten in the timeline. Although our work requires precision, the time buffer allocated to us is usually pushed to the very end. It requires working faster and avoiding any large mistakes in the workflow.

Q: What are the most valuable skills?
A: I will point out three key skills:

- Having a strong artistic eye. Mood, color, and composition all need to come together in the final image. A solid foundation in art, cinema, and photography can really elevate the quality of the work.
- Lighting is also very technical, as it pushes to understand the rendering pipeline, optimization, or color management, as examples. We often collaborate with Graphic Programmers or Technical Artists to improve our tools and visuals.
- Understanding and giving feedback. Lighting usually comes in late in production, meaning a lot of incoming feedback from other disciplines. It's important to filter, prioritize, and integrate what matters most. We also give feedback to help improve others' work, as lighting often brings the final visual together.

Q: What are some useful but optional skills?
A: Photography is a really good one to have. It's helping to observe and work with any details around us, focusing on shapes, silhouettes, compositing, colors, and exposure in a similar way to how we work in the engine. Scripting and coding are also a very good plus to be

able to understand the more technical part and to push the workflow further for the craft.

Q: How would you describe your typical working day?

A: I'm keeping my morning focused on the management side of my role: reviewing and noting feedback from others, identifying tasks to delegate to my team, and supporting anyone with technical issues or workflow questions.

I'll also be giving and receiving feedback, and collaborating with my team and other disciplines to align on new workflows or tools.

In the afternoon, I'll shift to the more creative side, focusing on lighting tasks for levels or cinematics.

Q: What's a common misconception about Lighting Artists?

A: Lighting art is more technical than what people have in mind. Placing lights on the level is just a part of the work itself. Some engines make it feel easy to light an entire level beautifully, but achieving the best game performance takes more time and effort to balance visual quality with optimization.

Q: What advice would you give to newcomers?

A: To develop his own art vision and show technical skills. It's great to exercise and try to reproduce other works from games or artists at first, but the Lighting Artist is always a very small craft, so having everyone with their own specialty and art styles is a plus for a team to develop new moods and new features for original games.

3.9 LEVEL ARTIST

Level artists are responsible for transforming rough blockouts from level designers into fully realized, visually compelling game environments. Through thoughtful asset placement, they enhance both the visual appeal and gameplay experience, ensuring the world feels immersive, cohesive, and alive – not only to look at but also to play through.

INTERVIEW WITH PHILIPPE ROUTHIER, SENIOR LEVEL ARTIST

Q: Tell us a bit about yourself.

A: My name is Philippe Routhier, I'm a Senior Level Artist at Ubisoft, and I started working in the game industry in 2008. I've had the opportunity to work as a level artist on many games, especially on the *Assassin's Creed* franchise (*Odyssey, Valhalla*, and *Shadows*). Outside of work, I'm also a musician: I have my own recording studio, and I especially enjoy punk-rock and metal music.

Q: What inspired you to pursue this career?

A: I have always been a gamer, and I have always been fascinated by virtual environments. It's been a revelation for me when I built my first level in Unreal Editor 1. I love creating immersive worlds or spaces that someone can move in, discover and enjoy.

Q: How did you get your first job as a Level Artist?

A: I got my first job as a Level Artist after spending 6 years working as a 3D Artist for projects in architecture, urban planning and marketing (still images, 360 images, animations). There was an opportunity to apply for a Level Artist role, and I needed something more creative, so I applied and got the job. However, after earning my degree in arts, I first worked as a Video Game Tester, Audio Designer and teacher for 3D Artists.

Q: What tools do you use?

A: Most of the work I do is with the help of an in-house game engine and its tools. I sometimes need a 3D software like 3ds Max, Photoshop for mock-ups, some generative AI for inspiration, etc. I also use some software for documentation, note-taking and task management, which is still an important part of my work.

Q: What's your favourite part of the job?

A: It's always fun to add details to an environment to make it more lively, interesting and realistic, but I particularly love composition. Giving structure to the space, creating interesting viewpoints, vistas, and reveals. I love organizing spaces and places so that they are interesting to visit. In an open world game, which I'm specialised in, the roads are as important as cities or any other locations.

Q: What's your least favourite?

A: I don't like it when tasks become too technical or repetitive for too long. I like it when I almost forget that I'm working in front of a computer and that my work is more creative and artistic than anything else.

Q: What are the most valuable skills?

A: Artistic talent, obviously . . . Knowing how to compose an image, organize space, create volumes, and make things readable and interesting. You also need to be well organized, have good team spirit and good communication skills. You need to make sure your needs are well understood and communicated, and to understand the needs of others. You have to work with a lot of people and make everyone happy despite the many constraints involved in creating a video game.

Q: What are some useful but optional skills?

A: Since we create worlds, a lot of general knowledge about any subject related to "real-life" world-building is really nice to have. Architecture, urbanism, interior design, geology, nature, etc. "Classic" art skills are also important, like general art theory, art history, drawing, painting, photography, lighting, cinema, etc. You also need to learn fast because tools are always changing and evolving.

Q: How would you describe your typical working day?

A: It really depends on the project and at what phase the project is (pre-production, production, etc.). Except maybe during the debug phase – when you're working through a list of bugs – each day can be quite different, which is quite awesome when you think about it.

Q: What's a common misconception about Level Artists?

A: Quite a lot actually! When I say I'm creating video games for a living, most people will think I'm a Programmer or an IT person. Now, when I explain that I'm a Level Artist, I often explain that my job is to create settings for games. That I create worlds, villages, landscapes, roads, but that I don't create the houses or the trees; I'm the one who places them to make the world interesting, logical and beautiful, and that a lot of people work with me on different aspects of that same world. Also, the Level Artist role might be different depending on the studio or project, as some will require more or less modelling tasks, for instance.

Q: What advice would you give to newcomers?

A: I can affirm that I have the most beautiful job in the world. Still, it can take a lot of skills, effort, and patience to get hired. There are many called but few chosen, but once you get there, it's totally worth it. Check what other people do, learn as much as you can, work hard and keep sharpening your skills. Once you get to a professional level, you'll get hired when the time comes. If you give up, it will never happen.

3.10 ANIMATOR

Animators bring characters, creatures, and objects to life through movement. They create animations for everything from walking, jumping, and fighting to facial expressions and cinematic sequences. Using keyframe animation or motion capture data, animators ensure animations feel responsive, believable, and aligned with gameplay. Their work is essential for delivering emotion, personality, and fluid interaction within the game world. Whether it's a hero gearing up for battle or a quirky side character tripping over their own feet, each animation tells a story and adds depth to the experience.

INTERVIEW WITH JOYCE MAKKER, ASSOCIATE DIRECTOR OF GAMEPLAY ANIMATION AT HANGAR 13

Q: Tell us a bit about yourself.

A: I'm Joyce Makker, I have 14 years of experience in 3D animation for videogames, including cinematics, gameplay animation for the player as well as enemies and other NPCs, motion capture directing, facial animation, and keyframing of creatures and characters. Previously, I was Associate Lead Animator for all body animations on *Top Spin 2K25*, and Lead Gameplay Animator on *Mafia: The Old Country*. Outside of work, I enjoy pencil and charcoal drawing, playing video games, and going on hikes.

Q: What inspired you to pursue this career?

A: I kind of fell into it actually! I wanted to do 2D art in either film or games since I was a teen, but when I tried 3D animation at uni, it just really clicked. It came naturally to me, and I fell in love with breathing life into characters. In hindsight, I believe it was because of my background in both drawing and ballet; animation is a combination of my passion for art and motion!

Q: How did you get your first job as an Animator?

A: My first job was an internship in animation for a small game studio. I was still attending university at the time. From there, I went on to freelance animation, and through freelancing, I got my first job at an AAA game studio.

Q: What tools do you use?

A: I primarily use MotionBuilder, as we use motion capture data for almost everything in our current project, but when I'm keyframing, I use Maya to animate. As I work in game development, I also work a lot in Unreal 5. It may be silly to mention, but as a Lead, I do work in Excel very frequently, as it's a powerful tool for organizing, analyzing, and communicating info and planning.

Q: What's your favourite part of the job?

A: My favorite part of my job as a Lead is making sure my team is able to run smoothly. There's nothing more satisfying than knowing that all Animators are doing what they do best. I take care of most of the planning and organization, while making sure the Animators have all the necessary information they need to do the job.

My biggest motivator is acquiring new knowledge and skills, both as a Lead and Animator. I don't think I'll ever stop learning in game development, there's no such thing as knowing everything, especially as the industry continues to evolve.

My absolute favorite is to consider the personality of a character and the context of a situation, and add that into an animation. That is when a character truly comes to life on screen.

Q: What's your least favourite?

A: Shooting my own video reference; acting is just not something I'm particularly good at, I'm afraid! Thankfully, a lot of our work is mocap-based, haha.

Q: What are the most valuable skills?

A: Of course, animation skills are important, including a thorough understanding of all animation principles. Additionally, for gameplay animation, it's important to understand what makes an action "feel good," which is a combination of controls, camera, responsiveness, readability, and fluidity.

For gameplay animation, collaboration is immensely important, so communication is one of our most valuable skills. We work closely with several other disciplines, and everyone has to align on the intent and approach, and collaborate on any adjustments and improvements as a feature takes shape.

Some technical skills are definitely required for gameplay animation. It allows us to break down a feature into the animations necessary, being able to troubleshoot reasons why our animations aren't doing what they're supposed to in-game, and it allows us to communicate better with technical disciplines.

Q: What are some useful but optional skills?

A: Having some knowledge of other related disciplines is highly beneficial. I have a secondary background in rigging as well as 2D art, and I'm very blessed to have animators on my team who lean either towards tooling, animation implementation, and motion capture, all of which make us a more well-rounded team!

Q: How would you describe your typical working day?

A: A lot of it is communication and organization. The animators are my top priority, so if they need anything, I will make time for them. I also make sure that the workload is manageable, so I'm checking everything is on track and whether I can do anything to support the animators. I talk to production and directors about priorities. As often as possible, at the end of the day, I play the game to see the latest and greatest, as well as check which areas of gameplay need more love and attention, and then I provide feedback to our animators as well as outsourcing partners.

Q: What's a common misconception about Animators?

A: I think people don't really know how many disciplines it takes to put gameplay animations on screen, even in game development! Riggers are responsible for creating the animatable characters we work with. Tech designers, engineers, and technical animators handle system development and feature implementation. A camera engineer steps in whenever a camera isn't pre-animated. Physical animation and cloth simulation also play a key role. And let's not forget the mocap actors and mocap crew! At times, we even collaborate with environment art, mission design, and character art on specific features.

Q: What advice would you give to newcomers?

A: Don't be afraid to jump into a game engine. I see a lot of animation reels with personal projects that are rendered in the animation software. Even if it was quite basic, any work in Unreal or Unity would automatically elevate your reel, because it shows that you have some interest and understanding of the pipelines beyond the animation software.

3.11 VFX ARTIST

Visual effects (VFX) artists are the ones who create effects like fire, explosions, weather, energy blasts, or any other effects needed for characters, environments, cinematics, and gameplay. They work with particle systems, animation, physics simulations, and sometimes shader programming to create effects that feel responsive and grounded in the game world.

This role requires a blend of technical precision and creative vision. VFX artists often collaborate closely with game designers to ensure their effects not only look great but also support gameplay clarity, feedback, and overall immersion.

INTERVIEW WITH FLORIAN GUILLAUD, SENIOR VFX ARTIST AT DON'T NOD

Q: Tell us a bit about yourself.

A: My name is Florian Guillaud, and I'm a Senior VFX Artist based in Paris, working in the video game industry on AA games for 8 years, now at DON'T NOD. I worked on *Life Is Strange 2*, *Banishers: Ghosts of New Eden*, and *Lost Records: Bloom and Rage*. I love climbing, gastronomy, painting miniatures, playing video games, animation, and reading fantasy books.

Q: What inspired you to pursue this career?
A: I wanted to do a lot of different things. Modeling, texturing, shading, animation, scripting, etc. And a VFX Artist does all of that. It's a multidisciplinary specialization.

Q: How did you get your first job as a VFX Artist?
A: I started as a 2D/3D Artist at Incarna Studios, where I did a lot of different tasks. But my focus was on the VFX of the game. Thanks to that, I succeeded in going to DON'T NOD as a Junior VFX Artist.

Q: What tools do you use?
A: I use Niagara, the Material Editor, and Blueprints from Unreal Engine. I also use Blender, Houdini, Substance, and Photoshop most of the time.

Q: What's your favourite part of the job?
A: Simply create VFX of all sorts. It's the most fun part of the role. It's kind of a puzzle for every effect, depending on the constraints we have to create them.

Q: What's your least favourite?
A: To think outside the box and communicate any potential issues to other departments to ensure our VFX are set up properly and work as intended. Since I'm shy, that part isn't always easy for me.

Q: What are the most valuable skills?
A: To be good at art. To be curious and wanting to learn and do all sorts of things. But most of all, to be adaptable, like a Swiss army knife.

Q: What are some useful but optional skills?
A: Having some basics in maths and physics, knowing the latest technologies and techniques, and being communicative.

Q: How would you describe your typical working day?
A: Starting with a sync with my Lead and meetings with other departments to be sure of what I have to do, and showing the current state of my work. Then, hours of making effects, but sometimes debugging too.

Q: What's a common misconception about VFX Artists?
A: People think creating VFX is quick and that we are just a post-production job that can fix and fill any gap in the game at the end. It's false. If we don't have a strong base (good environment, lighting, or animation, etc.), it will alter our effects, and it will require a lot of work.

Q: What advice would you give to newcomers?

A: As a VFX Artist, we do all kinds and styles of effects, and there are many ways to do it. So it's good to be curious and open-minded, having basics in a lot of stages (modeling, texturing, shading, lighting, scripting, etc.). To learn and improve as a VFX Artist, the web and its numerous tutorials are here to help, and the are a lot of free ones! Then, all you have to do is have a great portfolio and demo reel, and show that you are motivated.

3.12 UI ARTIST

User interface (UI) artists design and create the visual components that allow players to navigate games effectively. We're talking about everything from menus to heads-up display (HUD) elements, inventory screens, and dialogue boxes. The job isn't just about making things look good; it's about ensuring everything is intuitive, clear, and aligned with the game's aesthetic.

While UI artists focus on how things look and respond visually, they often collaborate with user experience (UX) designers, who define how players interact with those elements. In some cases – especially on smaller teams – the UI artist may take on UX responsibilities as well.

INTERVIEW WITH EDD COATES, LEAD
UI/UX ARTIST AND DESIGNER

Q: Tell us a bit about yourself.

A: My name's Edd Coates, a freelance UI/UX Designer with 12 years of experience in the industry. I've led the UI design on games like *Loco Motive*, *Prison Architect 2*, and *Golf With Your Friends 2*. I'm also the creator and founder of the Game UI Database – the games industry's leading resource for game UI – and author of *The Game UI Bible*. When I'm not obsessing over UI, I'm also a part-time composer for games and a singer-songwriter who performs around the country!

Q: What inspired you to pursue this career?

A: Funny enough, I wanted to be a game composer! However, I was dabbling in web and graphic design at the time, and one client asked me to design the UI for a mobile game. I enjoyed it, and that accidental job put me on the path to becoming a full-time UI Designer.

Q: How did you get your first job as a UI Artist?

A: I used to visit the GameDevClassifieds page on Reddit, as well as various Indie Game Developer groups on Facebook, and basically looked for any potential clients. They were pretty small jobs that didn't pay very much, but hey, I was working on video games, so I was very happy. Eventually, one client had me work on a mobile game with Drumond Park (the creators of the board game *Articulate*), which became my first "big break." The game wasn't great, but it gave me credibility to find other projects.

Q: What tools do you use?

A: Adobe Illustrator, Adobe Photoshop, and the Astute Plugin Suite.

Q: What's your favourite part of the job?

A: Whether it's a menu, HUD element, or even a pop-up window, UI is unique in that the player will almost always be interacting with *some* form of UI throughout the game. For this reason, my favourite part of being a UI/UX designer is the sheer amount of influence we can have! We shape the branding, responsiveness, and interaction of the product – all the important bits of the game! Properly utilised, a good UI Designer can single-handedly transform an entire game for the better.

Q: What's your least favourite?

A: Implementation. I don't think UI Designers should also have to handle implementation, especially if they're doing both UI and UX. It's a lot! But when unwilling programmers are left to implement UI, it can fall short, so we often have to do it ourselves. It's a boring necessity, sadly.

Q: What are the most valuable skills?

A: The ability to analyse existing interfaces. UI design is about solving problems, and many solutions already exist in other games. Knowing how to identify and apply them makes the design process much easier.

Q: What are some useful but optional skills?

A: Communication is just as important as being able to create the UI itself, especially when working in a large team. A lot of the time, we're expected to present our ideas to other team members or even defend them against opposing viewpoints.

So, being able to rationalise our ideas and present them in a compelling way is probably one of the most difficult parts of being a designer.

Q: How would you describe your typical working day?

A: A typical working day would just have me plugging away at part of the UI, to be honest! But which part really depends on where I am in the project. At the very start of a new project, I'll be collecting references to try to establish an art style. Shortly after that, I'll start wireframing screens, figuring out the UX, and establishing a structure for how the player moves through the menu system. Then I'll actually be creating the screens, and finally, I'll be overseeing the implementation process. But it's not quite as rigid as this, sometimes I might be doing more than one of these steps at the same time!

Q: What's a common misconception about UI Artists?
A: That we create buttons, HUDs, and menus. We're actually game designers, just more focused on interface systems. This means that in certain situations where it might be beneficial to use *less* UI or to present information in the world instead, it becomes really difficult for us to make these suggestions because we're not empowered to do so. The best UI teams to work with are always the ones that have the full backing, understanding, and respect of the studio!

Q: What advice would you give to newcomers?
A: Practice, practice, practice. Don't spend too long on a single project – just keep making things! Freelancing helped me grow quickly because I worked on a wide variety of projects in a short time. The art exploration phase is one of the most important in UI design, but usually only happens once per project. So, getting to do that over and over again was incredibly useful for my skills and confidence.

  The other piece of advice is to specialize. Many graduates submit portfolios full of art, web design, and a bit of UI. That approach can backfire, making you seem unfocused. This field is competitive. The most successful applicants are usually the ones who show the most passion for the role they're applying for. Don't be a dabbler, be a specialist!

3.13 CINEMATIC ARTIST

Cinematic artists bring scripted moments to life by crafting in-game cinematics and cutscenes that deliver emotional impact and narrative clarity. They use animation, camerawork, lighting, composition, and pacing to create sequences that feel cinematic, immersive, and aligned with the game's story and overall vision.

  On larger teams, previs artists handle early-stage planning by building rough storyboards and animations to block out timing and composition. Cinematic artists then refine and polish these sequences. On smaller projects, a single artist may take on both roles.

INTERVIEW WITH SHONA MARKUSEN,
CINEMATIC ARTIST

Q: Tell us a bit about yourself.
A: My name is Shona Markusen, and I'm a Cinematic Artist at Build a
Rocket Boy with 5 years of experience in AAA games. I have previously worked on titles such as *Little Hope*, *House of Ashes*, and *The
Devil in Me* of *"The Dark Pictures Anthology,"* as well as the flagship game *MindsEye* from former GTA Producer, Lezlie Benzies. In
my free time, I enjoy tabletop gaming, digital illustration, and hiking
with my beautiful rescue dog, Mia.

Q: What inspired you to pursue this career?
A: A love for games and visual storytelling.

Q: How did you get your first job as a Cinematic Artist?
A: I initially worked as an Assistant Camera Operator for a marketing company, but was on the lookout for something with a bit more
creative freedom. One day, I came across a post on LinkedIn for a
role as a "Camera Artist" at an AAA game studio making cutscenes.
Although I had not worked in a game engine before, the description
really piqued my interest as an avid gamer and aspiring Cinema-
tographer, so I was willing to learn and decided it was worth a shot
to apply. What I did not expect was an invitation to interview. As it
turned out, my showreel had shown promise, and they were looking
for candidates with a solid foundation in film language and storytelling.

Q: What tools do you use?
A: Unreal Engine, Motion Builder, and Premiere Pro.

Q: What's your favourite part of the job?
A: I absolutely love the problem-solving aspect that comes with balancing game mechanics and cinematics. Every day, there is a unique
challenge for me to work with and find a solution to that strikes the
balance between visually pleasing, narratively cohesive, and technically sound.

Q: What's your least favourite?
A: It's my job to make sure my cinematic cutscenes appeal to a wide
audience, and this is also the case internally. Because art as a whole is
so subjective, it can often be the case that what is approved by a team
Lead may not appeal to an Art Director, and it can take a long time to
iterate on something until everyone is happy. In this way, designing
cinematics is not always dissimilar to having a marketing client who
keeps changing the brief.

Q: What are the most valuable skills?

A: A solid understanding of film theory and visual language. It is absolutely essential to understand each shot you are crafting and why you are crafting it in that particular way. Technical skills in game engines and 3D software are no use if you cannot make intentional connections to a player and how they experience your game.

Q: What are some useful but optional skills?

A: With the exception of pre-vis, most Cinematic Artist roles will require some level of involvement with editing. Practice with software such as Premiere Pro is incredibly helpful as a part of your core skillset, but any free editing software will help you brush up on your fundamentals.

Q: How would you describe your typical working day?

A: The majority of my work consists of the placement and animation of cinematic cameras inside the game space. I will target a particular scene and set up cameras in my key locations and shot types (e.g., establishing shot, close-ups, etc.). Typically, I will do this in MotionBuilder, but in the past, I have worked exclusively in Unreal Engine. I will then slowly construct my edit using these key angles that I have framed up and start to add animations to bring movement and life into the scene. Once I am happy, the scene will go for review with the Art Director, and we will iterate as needed based on feedback and any bugs that may arise.

Q: What's a common misconception about Cinematic Artists?

A: That it is easy. The complexity of creating visuals that feel based on real-world logic would surprise you. Many people think that I can place a camera into an action scene, throw in some crazy tracking shots that fly around the protagonist, and it will automatically look awesome. I would say this is a pitfall that a lot of juniors will also fall into with their camera animations. Our audiences have been exposed to traditional film and media extensively, and the structures they follow have been ingrained into our minds. Placing a camera is definitely easy; you drag and drop, and you line it up for a pleasing angle. However, your shot could be on a boat, if the camera isn't "swaying" with the water like it would be if you were to take a physical camera rig onto a ship, your player will register that something feels slightly off and that can have massively detrimental affects on immersion and the overall enjoyability of the game.

Q: What advice would you give to newcomers?

A: Portfolio, portfolio, portfolio. Cinematic art is a massively visual job, so show off your skills! Keep making short films, play with different genres, and show off a variety of styles. It can be so difficult to break into your first role, but don't get disheartened; if your skills are there, you will eventually get noticed.

3.14 TECHNICAL ARTIST

Technical artists bridge the gap between art and programming. They build pipelines, create tools, write shaders, optimize assets, and solve technical problems. Depending on their focus, they might script tools to speed up workflows, use Houdini for procedural content generation, build advanced rigs for characters, or bring complex VFX to life.

Across the board, technical artists support artists directly – streamlining their workflows and making sure they can focus on creativity. They collaborate with multiple teams to improve processes and keep projects running smoothly. Simply put, they help ensure games look great and perform well.

INTERVIEW WITH MOHSEN TABASI, SENIOR TECHNICAL ARTIST AT SPLASH DAMAGE

Q: Tell us a bit about yourself.

A: I'm Mohsen Tabasi, a Senior Technical Artist at Splash Damage with over twenty years of bridging art and technology across games and animation. My career has let me contribute to projects like Ubisoft's *Skull and Bones*, *Star Ocean: The Divine Force*, and animated series, including *Not Quite Narwhal* and *Santiago of the Seas*. When I'm not solving technical art challenges, you'll find me tinkering with personal projects or enjoying time with my family.

Q: What inspired you to pursue this career?

A: I was always fascinated by the VFX in movies and 3D animations when I was young, which led me to start my career in the animation and film industry. After working in that space for a while, I realized that I was especially drawn to tools, workflows, procedural systems, and optimization. What really inspired me to pursue a career as a technical artist was the joy of solving creative problems through code and tools, and helping teams work more efficiently. It felt like the perfect balance between creativity and engineering, and that mix continues to keep me curious and excited every day.

Q: How did you get your first job as a Technical Artist?

A: I began my career as a rigger using Maya at an animation studio, but I soon discovered Houdini and became fascinated with procedural content generation. I spent a lot of time learning and experimenting with Houdini, which shifted my focus toward more technical and system-based work. When I decided to transition into the game industry, I applied for a Technical Artist position at Ubisoft Singapore. Fortunately, I received an offer, and that's how I started my journey in games.

Q: What tools do you use?
A: It's actually quite tricky to list a fixed set of tools or software for a technical artist, because the role is so broad and supports many different departments and task types. The tools I use are often directly tied to the game engine the project is built in, and they vary depending on what kind of challenges I'm tackling. For example, I'm currently working as a Technical Artist in Unreal Engine. For procedural content generation, I used to rely heavily on Houdini, but lately I've been focusing more on using Unreal Engine's native tools to develop custom systems. For automation tasks, Python is incredibly useful, especially when combined with Unreal's Editor Utility Widgets, which make it possible to create custom tools and streamline workflows right inside the editor.

Q: What's your favourite part of the job?
A: My favorite part of being a Technical Artist is building tools or systems that solve real production problems and make life easier for other artists. There's something really satisfying about seeing a team work faster or more creatively because of something I built. I also love how the role constantly pushes me to learn, whether it's new techniques, performance tricks, or better ways to bridge art and code. That mix of creativity, problem-solving, and collaboration is what keeps me excited.

Q: What's your least favourite?
A: If I had to pick a least favorite part of the role, it would probably be writing documentation. I absolutely understand how important it is, especially when working in a team or handing off tools, but it's definitely not the most exciting part of the process for me. I'd much rather be prototyping or problem-solving than formatting wiki pages. Still, I try to treat it as part of making my work truly useful and accessible to others.

Q: What are the most valuable skills?
A: The most valuable foundational skills for a Technical Artist are mathematics and programming. You don't necessarily need to go very deep into either, but having a solid understanding of both is essential, as most technical art tasks involve at least one of them.

It's also important to understand game engine pipelines, so you can troubleshoot and support other departments effectively. Knowing how assets move through the engine, from creation to final implementation, helps you troubleshoot issues, build better tools, and support artists and designers more effectively.

Also, the nature of a Technical Artist's role is constantly evolving, so it's important to stay up to date with new technologies, tools, and workflows. Being curious and willing to learn continuously is a big part of what makes someone successful in this role.

Q: What are some useful but optional skills?

A: I'd say art and creativity are two really valuable "nice-to-have" skills for a Technical Artist. Having a good artistic eye helps a lot, especially when working on procedural content generation tools that can produce art-directed results are always more effective and appreciated by artists. Creativity is equally important because most tech art problems don't have just one correct solution. Often, the best results come from thinking outside the box and designing solutions that not only solve the technical challenge but also enhance the visual or creative intent of the project.

Q: How would you describe your typical working day?

A: My day typically starts with a stand-up meeting to sync with leads and other tech artists. After that, I focus on tasks like developing shaders, optimizing assets, improving pipelines, or creating tools. No day is entirely predictable; supporting multiple departments (art, engineering, animation, VFX, etc.) means that unexpected issues often arise. Being the "bridge" between disciplines means adapting quickly and switching contexts as needed.

Q: What's a common misconception about Technical Artists?

A: That we're just artists who can script a bit, or programmers who occasionally touch art. In reality, it sits right at the intersection of art and engineering, and we need to understand both sides well. Whether that's building tools to speed up workflows, optimizing assets for performance, or solving complex visual challenges.

Q: What advice would you give to newcomers?

A: Focus on the fundamentals: math, programming, and understanding game engines. You don't need to be an expert in everything, but you should be comfortable enough to solve problems across art and code.

The tricky part? Tech moves fast. New tools, engine updates, and rendering techniques appear all the time, so staying curious and willing to learn is key. Play around with shaders, try automating boring tasks, and don't be afraid to break things while experimenting.

And since tech art is all about bridging gaps between teams, being a good communicator helps just as much as technical skills. At the end of the day, it's a job for tinkerers. If you like making things work better and look cooler, you'll fit right in.

3.15 GENERALIST

Instead of going all-in on just one specialization, generalists bounce between tasks: modeling characters, texturing environments, lighting, animation, and maybe even a bit of rigging or VFX if the project calls for it. They wear many hats, and somehow, they all fit. This versatility is especially valuable in small studios, startups, or indie teams, where adaptability outweighs specialization.

For newcomers, it can be a great way to figure out what you love most while still getting your hands dirty across the entire pipeline. Sure, it can be a lot. But if you enjoy variety, learning on the fly, and being the person who can jump in wherever needed, the generalist role could be perfect for you.

Education and Training

4

Now that you've gotten a feel for the industry and the most common specializations within game art, it's time to talk about the next big step: leveling up your skills. Maybe you're thinking about formal education, or maybe you want to learn the ropes on your own. There's no one right or wrong path here. The best way to learn depends on you. The options are as varied as the industry itself, so let's figure out what fits you best.

4.1 DEGREE PROGRAMS AND INSTITUTIONS

You might be wondering, "Do I really need a university degree?" The short answer: not necessarily. Plenty of successful artists out there are completely self-taught or learned through alternative means. That said, a formal education can still bring a lot to the table. As Figure 4.1 shows, having a games-related degree can significantly improve job prospects – nearly two-thirds of graduates landed jobs within a year, while less than a third managed the same without one.

A degree gives you structure – a clear path to follow, which can be a game changer if you struggle to stay motivated on your own. It's also a great way to build soft skills – things like communication, teamwork, and working under deadlines – that often get overlooked when you're learning solo.

And if you're thinking about working abroad, having a degree can open doors that might otherwise stay closed. Some opportunities require that piece of paper for visa sponsorship or to meet international hiring standards.

Speaking from experience, university gave me more than just knowledge. It kept me accountable and pushed me to keep leveling up, and the friendly competition with classmates was fuel for progress. I also stumbled into new interests through subjects I might not have explored on my own. And don't

DOI: 10.1201/9781003492320-4

overlook internships; doing one as part of your course curriculum can be a pivotal step for anyone trying to break into the industry.

Another huge bonus of formal education is the network you build. Your classmates will end up scattered throughout the industry, and they might be the very people who help you get your foot in the door. We'll go deeper into networking soon, but for now, if you thrive with structure and value in-person mentorship, a degree could definitely be worth it.

Of course, university isn't cheap, so it's important to weigh what you're getting against the investment. Let's break it down a bit more.

> "Techniques evolve, but the artistic foundations remain largely the same throughout the ages. Going to university is an excellent way to develop as an artist. What you learn there will remain useful throughout your life."
>
> – Philippe Routhier

> "I was lucky to find a great VFX program where the teachers taught me the logic behind CGI, not just how to use one tool. That foundation made it easier for me to learn anything in 2D or 3D."
>
> – Florian Guillaud

> "To be honest, I don't think attending university is necessary, as it's not a requirement for getting a job. However, I believe that immersing yourself in an academic environment can be valuable for personal growth. Additionally, sometimes it may be a requirement when applying for work visas."
>
> – Juan Novelletto

> "I stopped halfway through university as it seemed like a waste of money. You'll learn more from industry professionals and hands-on projects than through academic-heavy university courses. University is better for business, STEM, or fields like industrial design, where a degree is often required. No one has ever asked about my degree."
>
> – Damian Audino

> "As someone who looks at a lot of portfolios, I don't discount a person who hasn't attended a university. What is more important is that their portfolio is relevant to the job they are applying for."
>
> – Joyce Makker

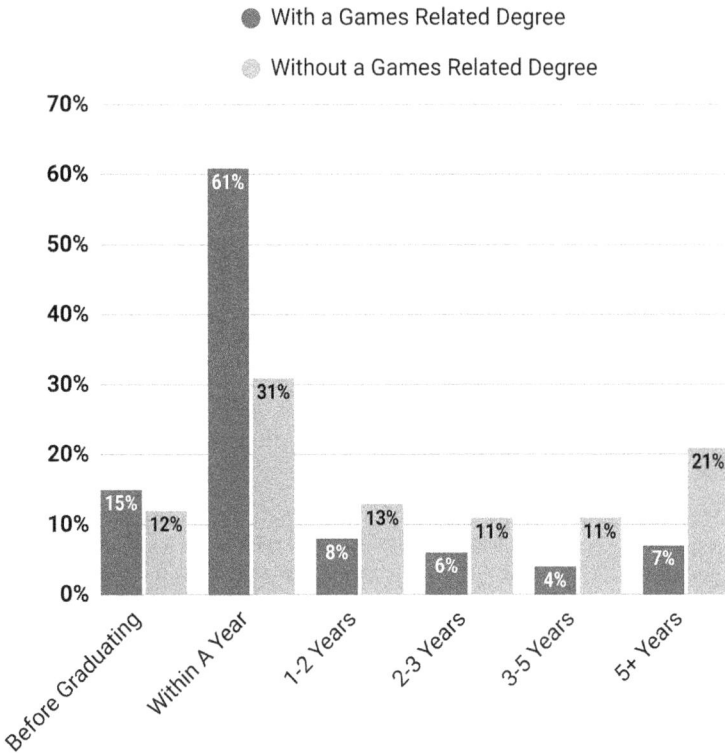

FIGURE 4.1   Time it took to land a game industry job, with or without a related degree.

Source: Based on data from Skillsearch's 2024/25 Salary and Satisfaction Survey, used with permission.

4.1.1 Research

The first thing to do when you're thinking about a degree is to find universities that actually offer a course in game art or something close to it. Not every program is the same, so you want one that fits your goals and gets you ready for the industry.

Start by checking out the program's reputation. Look up rankings, read what others say, and dig into portfolios from past students. Does the school have a track record of producing skilled game artists? Do they collaborate with game studios? What about internships? And do they bring in guest speakers from the industry?

Also, find out if they offer dedicated workspaces, or if you'll need to invest in your own high-spec PC or laptop. And what about the teachers – do they have real-world experience, and are they teaching the tools and workflows you'll actually use on the job? Lastly, check if their curriculum lines up with the skills you want to learn.

> *"I would mostly recommend going to university, if you know they have a quality course with teachers that had hands-on experience in game development. It'll help you learn and master the basics, stay organized, and work with a team on projects."*
>
> – Etienne Bednarz

> *"My main issue with a lot of game-related university courses is that they tend to focus on everything, rather than specialising in a specific aspect of game design. I'd say it's more valuable for the experience itself than for the actual content of the course. In my opinion, finding a mentor is far more beneficial."*
>
> – Edd Coates

4.1.2 Open Days

Open days are your best chance to get a feel for the university and figure out if it's the right fit. You get to walk the campus, check out the facilities, meet teachers and students face-to-face, and ask those questions that could make or break your decision. Here are a few good ones to have ready:

- What software and hardware will I have access to?
- Is there 24/7 access to labs or workspaces?
- How much of the course is hands-on versus theory?
- What kind of projects will I be working on throughout the course?
- How current is the curriculum with today's industry?
- Can I specialize in areas like character art, environment, or animation?
- Will I get to collaborate with other departments, like programming or design?
- Are there chances to work on collaborative projects with real clients?
- What kind of career support do they offer – portfolio reviews, internships?

- What's the process for getting internships – does the school help find them, or is it on me?
- Are there opportunities for mentorship or extra help if I struggle?
- What kind of feedback can I expect from teachers on my work?
- Are there opportunities to participate in game jams?
- Do they offer any scholarships or financial aid?
- What's the dropout rate like? Do most students finish the course?

And don't forget to explore the city too. Is it safe? Affordable? What's there to do besides study? You'll probably be living there for a few years, so it's worth making sure it fits you both in and out of class.

4.1.3 Reach Out to Graduates

One of the smartest moves you can make to gauge the quality of a program is to talk to alumni (that's just a fancy way of saying graduates), especially those with strong portfolios who've actually landed jobs in the industry.

Most schools have alumni groups or socials where you can reach out. These people have been through the whole thing and can give you real insights about what the course was like, what worked, what didn't, and how it set them up for the industry.

> *"It's essential to talk to graduates and have a good look at the curriculum before enrolling. I've seen many students graduate without the proper toolset to start working in the industry."*
>
> – Quinn Bogaerts

4.2 INTERNSHIPS AND GRADUATE SCHEMES

Internships and graduate schemes are one of the best ways to get your foot in the door. I know because that's exactly how I – and many of my former classmates – got into the industry.

They provide the opportunity to gain hands-on experience, improve your skills, and build the kind of connections that will last throughout your career. You'll be working on actual projects while learning from and collaborating with industry professionals. They can be the bridge between education and your first job, giving you a behind-the-scenes look at how a game studio runs and how projects come together.

Internships tend to be aimed at students or fresh graduates. Sometimes, they don't pay much (or at all), so it's important to be mindful of your finances before committing. But if you can manage it, the experience you gain is invaluable.

Graduate schemes are full time and structured. You'll usually get to rotate through departments, receive mentorship, and have a clearer path toward a permanent role. That said, specifics can vary by studio – some may focus more narrowly or have limited (or no) rotation depending on their size and structure.

Fair warning, though: these spots are just as competitive as actual jobs. But even if you don't land your dream job right away, every bit of experience helps you grow and figure out where you want to head next.

4.3 SELF-DRIVEN LEARNING

There's no single path to success. Like I've mentioned before, plenty of artists have made it by teaching themselves every step of the way.

That said, some argue that the term "self-taught" is a bit misleading, pointing out that no one truly learns in isolation. I think that's a fair point. Even if you're watching tutorials or reading articles, you're still learning from someone else. At a certain point, you're inevitably seeking out techniques, insights, and methods developed by others.

When I talk about being *self-taught*, what I really mean is learning at your own pace and focusing on what excites you most – whether that's character modeling, environment art, animation, VFX, or whatever you feel drawn to. This kind of freedom to tailor your learning isn't always something a formal program can offer, where the curriculum might be more rigid. And best of all? You don't need to break the bank on expensive tuition fees.

That kind of independence has its strengths, but it also demands a lot of discipline and consistency. You're the one who has to keep yourself on track. No one else is going to do it for you. You have to be your own biggest motivator.

That doesn't mean university is off the table. Even if you're in a formal program, pushing yourself to learn outside the classroom is important. When you combine self-driven learning with the structure of a solid formal education, you could get a winning combination that keeps you competitive and on top of your game.

> *"I was completely self-taught, with some mentoring from a friend."*
>
> – Edd Coates

> *"The vast majority of my learning was from other individuals or professionals. I went to an art school, but it only accounted for a small fraction of the true learning and growth comparatively."*
>
> – Dylan Mellott

> *"As a teenager, I started making mods for Half-Life 2 and maps for Counter-Strike Source, before going to a video game art school."*
>
> – Etienne Bednarz

4.4 PERSONAL PROJECTS

Want to grow as an artist? Personal projects are hands down one of the best ways to do it. It doesn't matter if you're still studying, taking online courses, or already working in the industry – this is how you stand out, get noticed, and keep on improving yourself. They give you space to put your skills to work, experiment with new stuff, and build a portfolio that reflects what you can do. You won't get far just watching tutorials or reading about workflows. At some point, you've got to get your hands dirty. After all, your portfolio is everything. It's the first thing employers check, and if it's not strong enough, you'll get passed over. That's the hard truth.

But it's not just about practice. Personal projects prove you can manage your time, stay motivated, solve problems, and see a project through from start to finish. Those are exactly the traits employers and clients are looking for.

And one piece of advice? Don't just stick with what you already know, but keep exploring and learning. If you're strong in one area, try stepping into something unfamiliar. Build an environment if you've only done stand-alone props. If you've focused solely on stylized work, tackle something more real-istic. The point isn't to be perfect – it's to grow. Exploring unfamiliar territory will broaden your knowledge and give you a better grasp of how everything connects in production.

So, if you've been putting off that personal project, take this as your sign to start. Push your limits, experiment, and create something that excites you. Who knows? Your next piece might just result in the breakthrough you've been waiting for.

4.5. COMMUNITIES AND PLATFORMS

Info overload is everywhere these days, but here's the upside: learning has never been more accessible. Beyond the endless stream of cute cat videos (no complaints there), the Internet is packed with courses, mentorships, and resources just waiting for you to dive in.

Some are free. Others cost money. And while it's not always backed by scholarships or student loans, what you're paying for often comes directly from artists working in the industry. That means you're getting the most up-to-date techniques and insights that can accelerate your growth and fast-track your career.

Below is a categorized list of popular platforms favored by artists – organized alphabetically within each category – to help you find what best fits your needs:

4.5.1 Mentorship and Career Development

Programs and schools that offer one-on-one mentorship, hands-on feedback, or structured boot camps to guide your growth and build a stronger portfolio. Many also offer online courses, so they often double as course platforms – which we'll look at in the next section.

- **Art Heroes 3D Art Academy** – An online art school specializing in 3D character art for games. It offers structured programs with live mentorship and feedback.
- **Beyond Extent** – A mentorship-driven community for environment artists, offering workshops, feedback, and resources focused on real-time game art and career development.
- **CG Master Academy (CGMA)** – A top-tier, industry-recognized school offering intensive, instructor-led courses and direct feedback from industry professionals.
- **CG Spectrum** – A certified online school with career-focused game art tracks and personalized mentorship in one-on-one or small-group formats.
- **Learn Squared** – It offers courses taught by leading artists, with downloadable project files, mentorship archives, and lifetime access.
- **M3DS Academy** – A game art academy offering courses, one-on-one mentorship, and career support.
- **Schoolism** – An online learning platform offering courses by industry artists, assignments, and optional personalized critiques.

- **Think Tank Training Centre** – A top-tier training school offering both online, on-campus, and hybrid mentorship programs in game art, 3D modeling, environment design, animation, and VFX.
- **Vertex School** – A career-focused online school offering bootcamp-style programs in game art and 3D production, with project-based learning and mentorship from industry professionals.

4.5.2 Course Platforms and Tutorials

Sites where you can find structured classes, (video) tutorials, and lessons taught by professionals.

- **CG Boost** – It offers project-based courses focused on Blender, stylized 3D art, and asset creation for games and animation.
- **CG Fast Track** – Focused on Blender, this platform provides beginner-to-intermediate tutorials with project-based lessons.
- **Coursera** – An academic-style platform providing university-level courses and certificates from reputable institutions. While dedicated game art courses are limited, you may find other related courses worth exploring.
- **Ctrl+Paint** – A free learning resource focused on digital painting fundamentals. Ideal for beginners, it breaks down complex topics into short, easy-to-follow videos.
- **Domestika** – A learning platform where industry professionals and an in-house team deliver project-based video courses in illustration, design, animation, 3D, and more.
- **Gnomon Workshop** – A professional training library from the prestigious Gnomon School, featuring detailed tutorials by leading industry artists.
- **Levelup Digital** – It offers high-quality, artist-led tutorials that teach professional workflows and techniques at your own pace.
- **LinkedIn Learning** – A professional-focused platform with intro-ductory creative and technical courses, often used by teams and companies. While dedicated game art courses are limited, related content such as design, software, or business skills may be worth exploring.
- **New Masters Academy** – While it is more fine-art-focused, it pro-vides strong fundamentals training in drawing, anatomy, and paint-ing that benefits any game artist.
- **Skillshare** – A subscription-based learning platform offering community-driven classes geared toward beginners and intermediate

learners. Though game art-specific content is limited, adjacent topics like illustration or digital painting may still be helpful.

- **Udemy** – A budget-friendly platform offering structured, one-time-purchase courses or subscription-based access to everything from 3D modeling to coding.
- **Wingfox** – A platform offering project-based tutorials and master classes on game art, character design, and digital painting. Not all courses are in English; however, many include English subtitles.

4.5.3 Art Resource Marketplaces

Places where you can buy art assets, tutorials, tools, and reference materials.

- **3D Scan Store** – A marketplace offering high-quality photogrammetry scans and 3D assets for game developers and artists.
- **ArtStation Marketplace** – A platform for purchasing and selling digital art resources, including brushes, tutorials, 3D models, and more. As of writing, there are plans for it to be merged into Fab Marketplace as part of Epic Games' unified ecosystem.
- **Cubebrush** – A marketplace for artists to buy and sell tutorials, assets, and tools, with a focus on game development and concept art.
- **Fab Marketplace** – Epic Games' new unified storefront combining Unreal Engine Marketplace, Quixel Megascans, ArtStation Marketplace, and Sketchfab. It offers 3D models, VFX, materials, tools, and more.
- **FlippedNormals** – A curated marketplace where professionals sell tutorials, tools, and 3D assets tailored to the CG and game art industry.
- **Gumroad** – A storefront platform where individual creators sell tutorials, tools, brushes, and models.

4.5.4 Industry Insight and Inspiration

Websites and blogs offering breakdowns, interviews, workflows, and deep dives into real production environments.

- **ArtStation Magazine** – Official editorial arm of ArtStation; it shares interviews, tutorials, tool updates, and community challenges, spotlighting what's trending in digital art.

- **3dtotal** – Starting out as a digital art resource site, 3dtotal has evolved into a leading publisher of art books. It also features interviews, project breakdowns, tutorials, and a curated blog. It is known for its high-quality art books, anatomical figures, and articles.
- **BlenderNation** – Publishes daily Blender art, tutorials, and community projects; an excellent resource for artists looking for trends, knowledge, and inspiration.
- **Concept Art World** – A resource site featuring concept art, artist spotlights, and links to interviews, books, and tools.
- **Experience Points** – This site offers in-depth articles, artist showcases, and podcasts that share real-world insight into the art and game industry.
- **GDC Vault** – An archive of free and paid Game Developers Conference (GDC) talks. It features in-depth breakdowns from top studios on pipelines, tools, and workflows.
- **Game Developer (formerly Gamasutra)** – Long-running site with deep dive articles and post-mortems.
- **GameTextures Blog** – It focuses on material and texture creation, workflows, and updates tied to their library, with occasional articles for anyone working with textures.
- **Into Games** – A UK-based organization offering career guidance, role breakdowns, and interviews to help aspiring professionals enter the games industry.
- **Pixologic/ZBrush Blog** – Official blog featuring sculpting showcases, artist spotlights, and detailed process write-ups; it is great for ZBrush-focused inspiration.
- **The Gnomon Workshop Blog** – Companion to Gnomon's training platform; it features interviews, behind-the-scenes posts, and technique breakdowns by professional artists.
- **Unreal Engine Blog** – Epic Games' official dev blog with artist interviews, case studies, and visual showcases of Unreal projects.
- **Unity Blog** – It covers pipeline tips, workflows, and artist-friendly tools in Unity projects.
- **80.lv** – An industry-focused hub with interviews, project breakdowns, tool rundowns, and production insights.

4.5.5 Showcase and Discovery Platforms

Sites for sharing work publicly, getting inspired by the work of others, and connecting with the broader creative community – some of which also double as portfolio hosts (see Chapter 7 for a broader look at portfolio platforms).

- **ArtStation** – Portfolio site at its core, with some social and educational features like comments, blogs, and a marketplace for assets and tutorials.
- **Behance** – A creative portfolio platform by Adobe that enables discovery and appreciation, with light social features like likes, follows, and comments.
- **DeviantArt** – One of the oldest general-purpose art communities.
- **Dribbble** – More focused on UI/UX, but useful for game menus, HUDs, and unique interface designs.
- **Pinterest** – A visual discovery platform for gathering and sharing reference boards. It's widely used by artists for inspiration, mood exploration, and style research.
- **Shadertoy** – A community platform for creating and sharing real-time generative shaders; a rich source of inspiration and technical insight for graphics artists.
- **The Rookies** – Designed for students and emerging artists, with contests, ranking features, and exposure opportunities geared toward career building.

4.5.6 Communities and Feedback Hubs

Focused, in-depth discussion spaces for critiques, problem-solving, and peer feedback. They're structured more like traditional message boards than social feeds.

- **Autodesk 3ds Max Forum** – Official Autodesk community for 3ds Max users, featuring support threads, feature discussions, and user projects. Ideal for troubleshooting modeling, workflows, and plug-ins.
- **Autodesk Maya Forum** – The official Autodesk Maya community forum, covering everything from modeling and animation to scripting, plug-ins, and troubleshooting in production workflows.
- **Autodesk MotionBuilder Forum** – The official Autodesk MotionBuilder community forum for virtual cinematography and character animation. Users ask questions about motion capture cleanup, animation pipelines, and software troubleshooting.
- **Blender Artists** – A forum dedicated to Blender users, covering everything from modeling and sculpting to rendering and game asset creation.
- **Krita Artists Forum** – A community for users of Krita (open-source painting software), where digital painters and texture artists share work and tips.

- **Marvelous Designer Forum** – The official support community and user forum for Marvelous Designer. You'll find questions and answers on garment construction, simulation settings, export workflows, and troubleshooting.
- **Pixel Joint** – A dedicated community for pixel art and game sprites. It includes forums, galleries, and regular challenges.
- **Polycount** – A long-standing forum for game artists focused on critique, production workflows, and technical discussion.
- **Real Time VFX** – A forum centered on real-time VFX for games, with discussions on particles, shaders, simulations, and technical workflows.
- **Reddit** – While not a traditional forum, many art-related subreddits (like r/gamedev, r/3Dmodeling, or r/learnart) function as discussion hubs and feedback spaces.
- **SideFX Houdini Forums** – The official community portal for Houdini users, featuring threads, help sections, and software discussions.
- **TopoGun Forum** – A dedicated forum (hosted on Reallusion's site) and community discussion for TopoGun users. Artists frequently discuss edge-flow techniques, baking workflows, and efficiency tips.
- **Unreal Engine Forums/Unity Forums** – Official engine forums that include strong communities for game developers and artists.
- **ZBrushCentral** – A specialized community for ZBrush users, offering critiques, tutorials, and showcase threads.

4.5.7 Social and Live Communities

You likely know these already, but they're still among the most valuable platforms for artists to share their work, build an audience, get feedback, and stay current with trends.

- **Bluesky** – A newer microblogging platform similar to Twitter/X, where many artists are starting to share their work and connect.
- **Discord** – Real-time chat and voice servers for everything from feedback and critique to mentorship and art jams. It's a great place to find niche groups, and many courses now include dedicated Discord servers for communication and support.
- **Facebook** – Facebook hosts active groups for a wide range of art niches. It is useful for community support, sharing work, getting feedback, and casual networking.

- **Instagram** – A go-to platform for artists to share work, grow a following, and explore trending techniques through reels and hashtags.
- **TikTok** – Popular for short-form tutorials, time lapses, and art challenges. It is fast-paced but surprisingly educational in small doses.
- **X (formerly Twitter)** – A fast-moving feed where many game developers and artists share WIPs, breakdowns, job tips, and industry news. It is not ideal for deep feedback but excellent for staying plugged in.

Feedback

5

Let's be honest – feedback isn't always easy. Sometimes, it stings. Sometimes, it's vague. And sometimes, it just throws you off balance. But if you want to grow as a professional, learning how to take feedback well is a must. In an industry that thrives on collaboration and iteration, dealing with feedback – whether you're receiving or giving it to someone else – is something every artist has to face. By understanding the dynamics of feedback, you'll not only grow as an artist but also become a more effective team player.

5.1 TAKING FEEDBACK

Taking feedback well is one of the most important soft skills you can develop as an artist. But how should you handle it when someone critiques your work?

Start with an open mind. It's normal to feel a bit defensive, especially if you've poured a lot of time into something. But remember: the feedback is about the work, not you. (Unless it's about your attitude or how you collaborate – in that case, listen up.) How you respond to critique and interact with others can shape your career just as much as any of your other skills.

When feedback comes in, your job is to listen carefully. Don't jump in with excuses or explanations – just hear them out. If something's unclear, ask for clarification. Simple questions like "Can you be more specific?" or "What should I focus on improving?" show openness and help ensure you understand what's being asked.

If something rubs you the wrong way, pause – not to stay silent but to respond with intention. It's okay to take a breath, ask for clarity, and give yourself a moment to process. If you're not sure how to respond right away, it's perfectly fine to say, "Let me think about that and get back to you." That way, you stay engaged without reacting impulsively.

DOI: 10.1201/9781003492320-5

After thinking it over, if the feedback still doesn't sit right, follow up and have a respectful conversation. Maybe you misunderstood, or maybe they did. Either way, it's better to clear the air than let frustration build. Taking feedback well isn't about staying quiet – it's about communication, curiosity, growth, and working together to achieve the best possible result.

Whether or not you agree with the feedback, you always want to stay respectful. Even if it's blunt or poorly delivered, keeping your cool shows professionalism – and over time, that builds trust.

In reality, you'll get feedback from all directions: art directors, leads, teammates, clients, and sometimes total strangers online. Not all of it will be useful. Some will help, some won't, and occasionally, you'll hear completely opposite opinions. Learning to filter feedback is just as important as receiving it.

If it comes from your art director, lead, or another senior team member, you're expected to act on it. If it's from another department, remember they may not have full context – so check with your lead before making big changes.

For personal work, the choice is yours. But even then, it's worth listening. An outside perspective might catch something you missed or offer a new way to look at your work.

Once you've taken in the feedback, step back and think it through. Not every critique will align with your goals – and that's okay. Your job is to figure out which changes will actually improve the work. What will have the biggest impact? What's worth prioritizing?

When it's time to apply the feedback, break it down into manageable steps. Big changes can feel overwhelming, but small adjustments – a few tweaks, adjusting your workflow, or rethinking your approach – add up. Whatever it looks like, take it one step at a time.

After making progress, check back in with the person who gave you the feedback. It shows you value their input and are serious about improving. A quick follow-up can also help confirm you're heading in the right direction – or steer you back before you go too far off track.

And don't forget to say thank you. Someone took time out of their day to help you grow. That's worth acknowledging. A quick "thanks, I appreciate it" shows you respect their input and helps build trust. Simple, but powerful.

5.2 PROVIDING FEEDBACK

Giving feedback is just as important a skill as receiving it, and doing it well isn't always easy. You don't want to crush someone's confidence, but at the same time, you also don't want to sugarcoat things so much that your critique becomes useless.

The sweet spot is balance. Be honest, be clear, and be encouraging.

Saying stuff like "This doesn't work" or "Make it better" isn't going to help anyone. Instead, focus on *what* needs improvement, *why* it matters, and *how* it can be improved. The goal is to help the person grow, not to tear them down.

Also, not everyone reacts to criticism in the same way. Some prefer blunt honesty, while others need a more careful approach. Understanding these differences is important to giving feedback that resonates and motivates.

Try to frame your critique around solutions, not just problems. Instead of saying, "This character feels off," try, "The proportions seem a bit unbalanced – maybe tweaking the forearm length could improve the overall anatomy." See the difference? Same message, but more useful.

A good approach is to start with a positive, share the critique, and follow it with a clear suggestion for improvement. If feedback is all negative, it's demotivating. If it's all positive, it's not helpful. Find that middle ground.

And heads up: especially in public spaces like socials, it's best to ask if someone wants feedback first. Even the best critique can feel harsh if it's unwanted. In the workplace, feedback is expected, but respect is always important.

When critiquing a colleague, think of it as collaboration, not judgment. Your feedback should move the project forward and elevate its quality, not create friction.

At the end of the day, feedback is about growth. So before you share your thoughts, ask yourself: am I being specific? Constructive? Actually helpful? If the answer is yes, you're doing it right.

5.2.1 Different Ways to Provide Feedback

Feedback can take many forms, and what works for one artist might not work for another. Using the right approach can make your critique more effective and engaging. Here are some common methods to consider:

1. **Written Feedback** – A straightforward, organized written critique is often very effective. Break it down into what's working well, what could be improved, and specific suggestions on how to make those improvements.
2. **Verbal Feedback** – Whether in-person or over a video call, real-time conversations let you clarify points and answer questions on the spot. Some platforms even have paint-over tools where you can

draw directly on the shared screen to highlight exactly what you mean.

3. **Paintovers** – A quick visual critique where you paint directly on the artwork to demonstrate potential changes or improvements.

4. **Before/After GIFs** – Create a simple animated GIF that flips between the original piece and your suggested adjustments. It's an engaging way to visualize the impact of the changes.

5. **Markup and Notes** – Use annotation tools to circle areas that need work and add brief notes explaining what and why.

6. **Reference Comparisons** – Show side-by-side comparisons with reference images so the artist can see how their work stacks up and where tweaks might help.

7. **Video Feedback** – Record your screen while talking through your critique and demonstrating fixes. It's a more personal, interactive way to guide improvements.

8. **Layered Files** – If you have access to the working file – like a PSD or ZBrush file – you can leave notes or example tweaks on separate layers directly inside the file.

5.3 SHARING YOUR WORK

One of the biggest hurdles you'll face is learning to share your work. It's so easy to fall into the trap of thinking your work has to be perfect before anyone else sees it. The truth is, no matter how skilled you become, perfection is a moving target. It's something you'll never fully "reach." What matters most is progress and learning along the way. That's why feedback is one of the most valuable tools you'll have at your disposal throughout your entire career.

As you know by now, game development is a collaborative effort. Unless you're flying solo, you're rarely working in isolation. Whether it's code, design, art, or sound, everything must fit within the larger vision of the game. By sharing your work early, you open the door for others to jump in and help make sure your art fits into that unified vision.

It's only natural to feel protective of your creations. But keeping your work to yourself for too long can actually slow you down. Without fresh eyes, it's easy to miss little things that throw off the overall direction or create inconsistencies. You don't have to have all the answers alone. By sharing your work, you give others the chance to help you see things from a new perspective, which can lead to improvements you hadn't thought of.

Over time, you'll learn that feedback is part of the process. So don't hesitate to share your work and ask for input. The more you do it, the faster you'll grow as an artist.

5.4 ATTACHMENT

It's also easy to get attached to the work you create, especially when you've poured a lot of time and effort into it. Feeling proud of what you make is only natural. But the reality of working in a studio is that none of your work actually belongs to you. Every model, texture, concept, or animation you create is the company's property.

Does that mean you shouldn't care? Absolutely not. You should always aim to do your best work. But getting too emotionally invested can make every revision, piece of feedback, or big change feel like a personal attack. And that's a quick path to burnout. Sometimes, a piece you've spent weeks on gets scrapped or passed to someone else. It's not about your talent – it's just the nature of the job (and often, bad planning).

The best artists learn to stay emotionally detached from the final outcome while still putting passion into the process. That mindset helps you adapt, stay professional, and keep your focus on the bigger picture. At the end of the day, your job is to create what's best for the game and not to hold on tightly to every piece as if it were your personal work.

Networking and Events

6

Networking isn't just about handing out business cards. It's about building genuine, meaningful relationships. Relationships that are built on mutual respect, trust, and a shared passion for the craft.

If you're serious about a career in game development, making a name for yourself should be high on your priority list – and that starts with networking. The game industry is a tight-knit community, and getting yourself involved is one of the best ways to unlock new opportunities, get feedback, and build your support system.

6.1 GAME CONFERENCES AND EVENTS

Let's first talk about the industry events themselves. Whether it's big events like PAX or Gamescom or more developer-focused conferences like GDC or Develop:Brighton, these events are full of opportunities to connect with industry professionals, learn new things, and keep up with the latest trends. Alongside technical talks, case studies, and panel discussions, you'll also find exhibitions and studio booths, where recruiters and developers are available to engage directly with attendees. Yes, these events take time, energy, and money, but trust me, they're absolutely worth it. And the best part? You don't always have to travel across the globe; there are plenty of events happening closer to home or even online. Of course, there are far more conferences and events than I can list here, but here's a quick look at a few you might find worth attending:

6.1.1 General Conferences

- **Animex** – Middlesbrough, UK
  A long-running festival focused on animation, VFX, and games.

DOI: 10.1201/9781003492320-6

- **Develop:Brighton** – Brighton, UK
  A game development conference, with sessions on art, animation, and career growth alongside tech and design talks.
- **Digital Dragons** – Kraków, Poland
  One of Europe's major game conferences, offering talks and workshops across game design, art, and business.
- **EGX** – London, UK
  The UK's flagship gaming expo, featuring upcoming releases, industry panels, and esports.
- **Game Access** – Brno, Czech Republic
  An annual conference for game developers, featuring talks, workshops, and showcases focused on game development, including art, design, and animation.
- **Game Industry Conference (GIC)** – Poznań, Poland
  Held alongside Poznań Game Arena, GIC offers developer talks, art-focused panels, and career matchmaking.
- **The Game Awards** – Los Angeles, USA
  The premier annual event celebrating the best in video games, featuring awards, exclusive premieres, and industry highlights.
- **Gamescom** – Cologne, Germany
  One of the largest gaming events globally, with a strong industry presence through its Devcom conference, offering talks and networking for game developers and artists.
- **Game Developers Conference (GDC)** – San Francisco, USA
  One of the biggest game industry conferences, featuring talks, workshops, and an expo covering all aspects of game development, including art, animation, and visual effects.
- **Montreal International Game Summit (MIGS)** – Montreal, Canada
  A key event in North America with a strong focus on AAA development, art, design, and tech. Ideal for networking with major studios and hearing from experienced developers across all disciplines.
- **Nordic Game Jam** – Copenhagen, Denmark
  An annual 48-hour nonprofit game jam that brings together developers and artists to explore bold ideas, push creative boundaries, and experiment with innovative game design in a fast-paced, collaborative setting.
- **Nordic Game** – Malmö, Sweden
  This international conference brings together developers from around the world for sessions on game design, art direction, and industry trends. An additional autumn edition takes place in Helsinki, Finland.
- **Penny Arcade Expo (PAX) Series** – Various Locations
  A series of events across the United States and Australia, featuring

indie game showcases, panels, and networking for developers, including artists.

- **Pocket Gamer Connects** – Various Locations (Global)
A mobile-focused game dev conference series held in cities like London, Helsinki, and Toronto. It includes talks on art, game design, and monetization for mobile and indie developers.
- **Promised Land** – Łódź, Poland
A creative arts festival focused on game development, animation, and both digital and traditional art. It features industry talks, portfolio reviews, and hands-on workshops with industry professionals.
- **Reboot Develop** – Dubrovnik, Croatia
A rapidly growing game developer conference that offers talks, panels, and workshops focused on game design, art, and business.
- **SIGGRAPH** – Various Locations (North America and Asia)
The top event for computer graphics and interactive techniques, especially valuable for VFX and technical artists.
- **Tokyo Game Show (TGS)** – Tokyo, Japan
While primarily consumer-focused, it includes industry and development sessions, some of which touch on game art and design.
- **Unite (Unity Conference)** – Various Locations
Hosted by Unity, this event focuses on game development, including 3D art, animation, and rendering techniques.
- **Unreal Fest** – Various Locations and Online
For anyone working with Unreal. It covers everything from rendering to animation to VR, with practical sessions for artists and game developers.
- **Yorkshire Games Festival** – Bradford, UK
A regional festival highlighting careers and creativity in games, featuring talks and workshops on development, art, and animation.

6.1.2 Artist-Focused Events

- **Annecy International Animation Festival** – Annecy, France
The world's leading event dedicated entirely to animation, showcasing films, series, and creative work across all styles and formats.
- **Blender Conference** – Amsterdam, Netherlands
A dedicated conference for Blender users, covering 3D modeling, animation, and game-related workflows.
- **Concept Art Awards and Workshops** – California, USA
Typically held alongside LightBox Expo, this event honors concept art across games, film, and TV, featuring expert-led workshops and insightful panels.

- **CTN Animation Expo** – California, USA
  An annual event in Burbank, California, that connects animation professionals and emerging artists through panels, workshops, and portfolio reviews.
- **IAMAG Master Classes** – Various Locations
  An event featuring talks from some of the best concept artists, illustrators, and game industry professionals.
- **LightBox Expo** – California, USA
  A convention designed for artists in games, animation, and illustration.
- **Trojan Horse Was a Unicorn** (**THU**) – Various Locations (Global)
  An artist-focused event for digital artists in games, animation, and film, offering networking, mentorship, and inspiration.
- **VIEW Conference** – Turin, Italy
  A global event covering VFX, animation, game development, and immersive media. It includes sessions on digital art, storytelling, and technical innovation.
- **ZBrush Summit** – Los Angeles, USA, and Online
  A dedicated annual event for ZBrush users, focusing on sculpting for games and film.

6.2 LOCAL MEETUPS

If the big industry events feel a little out of reach, don't worry – many cities also have local meetups you might find just as valuable. These are more casual gatherings often held in cafes, bars, coworking spaces, or restaurants. No badges, no booths – just a bunch of passionate people talking art, games, and everything around it. You'll find a mix of industry professionals, aspiring artists, students, and passionate game enthusiasts. It's casual, approachable, and way less intimidating than a giant expo hall.

What makes local meetups especially appealing is their relaxed, easygoing atmosphere. Unlike large-scale events that can feel overwhelming or impersonal, these smaller get-togethers make it easier to strike up conversations, ask questions, and connect with others more naturally.

And if it's hosted in a bar? No pressure – there's zero expectation to drink. Coffee, tea, soda – it's all good. The focus is on shared passion, not what's in your glass.

If you're looking to grow your network, exchange ideas, stay inspired, or simply surround yourself with like-minded people, local meetups are a great place to start. You never know who you'll meet.

6.3 ONLINE COMMUNITIES

Back in Chapter 4, we talked about how online communities can be a valuable resource for learning and personal growth. But what I didn't touch on is how these communities can also be great for networking.

If you're more of a stay-at-home, cozy vibe person, you've got tons of online spaces to tap into. From forums to Discord servers, there's something for everyone.

When you're just starting out, my advice is to pick one or two communities and really take the time to get to know the people there. Sure, you could sign up for every single group out there (more networks = more chances, right?), but at first, it's easier to form meaningful connections by focusing your energy on just a handful. Down the line, when you're ready, you can always branch out and grow your circle bigger.

Not sure where to start? Just head back to the *Communities and Platforms* section in Chapter 4, where I've already rounded up the most popular spots for you to jump in.

6.4 GAME JAMS

Game jams are intense, fast-paced events where programmers, designers, and artists come together to create a game in a ridiculously short amount of time (usually in just a few days) – all within a set theme or topic. And honestly, they can be a lot of fun too.

For game artists, game jams are a fantastic way to experiment with new styles, sharpen your workflow, and improve your collaboration skills – all while working against the clock. They're also great for meeting other creatives and developers, which can lead to future collaborations or even job opportunities.

The best part is that game jams are open to everyone. Whether you're a seasoned professional or just starting out, there's a spot for you. While many happen in person, there are plenty of online game jams too, so you can participate from wherever you are. Some schools even include them as part of their curriculum, giving students real hands-on experience in rapid game development.

If this sounds like something you'd enjoy, try searching for game jams near you or exploring online options, and give it a try. Trust me, it's worth it and will also look great on your CV.

> *"I've done several Game Jams. I highly recommend them. It's a great chance to meet other developers and experience working on something together."*
> — Dylan Mellott
>
> *"I don't really recommend game jams if you're not making time for rest or other activities. Skipping sleep and overworking isn't reflective of how things function in a real job."*
> — Florian Guillaud
>
> *"I would absolutely recommend game jams. They are great fun and can spark reinvigorated passion for the work we do."*
> — Quinn Bogaerts

6.5 NETWORKING ADVICE

Now that you know *where* to network, the next big question is: *how* do you actually do it? The truth is, networking is a skill like any other. The more you practice, the better you'll get at it. And if you're more on the introverted side, I understand putting yourself out there can feel intimidating. I've felt the same way, and honestly, I still do sometimes.

But here's the thing: you don't need to be the most outgoing person in the room to make meaningful connections. It's about showing up, being genuine, and finding common ground with others in the industry.

To take some of the pressure off, I've put together some practical tips to help ease the nerves and get the most out of networking:

6.5.1 Be Yourself

People are naturally drawn to those who are genuine. So instead of trying to impress others with a rehearsed pitch or trying to say what you think others want to hear, just be yourself.

One of the biggest mistakes is approaching conversations with a set agenda. While it's important to have goals, trying to force interactions into a script can make you come off as insincere. Instead, stay present, listen carefully, and respond genuinely. The best connections happen through honest conversations, not rehearsed lines.

6.5.2 Be Approachable

People are far more likely to approach you if you come across as open and friendly. Simple things like a smile, eye contact, and open body language send powerful signals that you're approachable.

Try to avoid crossing your arms or hunching over – it might seem small, but it can make you look closed off or uninterested. Instead, keep your arms relaxed and use open gestures.

And please, put your phone away – unless you're using it to take notes or to show something relevant during the conversation. Being fully present shows respect for the person you're talking to and for the conversation itself.

6.5.3 Overcoming Anxiety

Networking can feel intimidating, especially if you struggle with social anxiety. First, accept that feeling anxious is completely normal, even for the most seasoned of us, so don't let it control you.

One way to manage anxiety is through preparation. The more prepared you are, the more confident you'll feel. Having a few questions in mind, like "What's your latest project?" or "How did you get started?", helps ease into conversations without scrambling for words. It also helps to practice a brief intro about who you are, what you do, and what you're looking for. But like I mentioned earlier, be careful not to sound too rehearsed, as it can come off as forced or unnatural. Find that sweet spot between being prepared and staying flexible enough to let the conversation flow naturally.

Another useful technique is to focus on the other person. Often, we get anxious because we're too focused on how we're coming across or whether we're saying the right thing. Instead, shift your focus to listening and showing interest in the other person's work or experience.

And if attending events solo feels overwhelming, bring a friend. A familiar face can boost your confidence and make networking less stressful.

Remember, you don't need to talk to everyone. One meaningful conversation is often enough to calm your nerves and build confidence for the rest of the event.

6.5.4 Communication

When speaking with others, keep your message simple and direct. Instead of rambling, try to articulate your thoughts in a way that's easy for the listener to follow. Be mindful of your tone and pace. Listening is just as important. Engage with the other person, show interest, and respond thoughtfully. While we touched on body language earlier in the context of being approachable, it also plays an important role in communication. Eye contact, open posture, and natural gestures help reinforce your message and how it's received.

6.5.5 Quality over Quantity

When you meet someone new, try shifting your mindset from "What can I get?" to "What can I learn?" Ask thoughtful questions, be genuinely curious, and don't treat the conversation like a checklist. Don't just talk to people for the sake of collecting contacts, but to get to know them on a deeper level.

Meaningful relationships don't happen overnight. They take time and effort. So follow up. Stay in touch. Offer help when you can. The strongest connections are built on trust and mutual support.

6.5.6 Online Networking

In today's digital age, networking isn't just face-to-face anymore. The Internet lets you connect with people from all around the world – people you'd probably never meet otherwise. Pretty cool, right?

When you reach out, personalize your message. Nobody likes receiving a bland, copy-and-paste message that feels like it's been sent to everyone. Instead, take a moment to introduce yourself, mention what caught your eye about their work, and let them know what you'd love to chat about. Keep it concise and respectful of their time. A thoughtful message is far more likely to get a positive response than a generic one.

That said, online networking isn't just about DMs. It's about showing up. Don't just scroll, but join the conversation. Share your thoughts. Post your work. Connect with people who care about the same things you do.

6.5.7 Helping Others

Instead of only asking for favors or opportunities, think about how you can contribute to others in your community. That might mean making introductions, sharing useful resources, offering feedback, reposting someone's work, or simply showing up to support others – whether that's attending their talk, exhibition, or game launch.

By helping others, you're not only building your own network but also positioning yourself as a valuable resource. And you know what? That can often open the door to unexpected opportunities for you, too.

But let's not forget, a healthy network requires balance. Networking is a two-way street. Your connections should be mutually beneficial, so make sure you're not only giving but also letting others help *you* when needed.

6.5.8 Business Cards

While they might seem like a relic from the past, business cards are still incredibly valuable when it comes to networking. They provide a simple, tangible way to leave a good impression and make it easy for others to reach out to you (especially if, like me, you have a surname that's easy to misspell). A well-designed card reflects your professional brand and should include your name, job title, contact details, and website.

A helpful tip someone once shared with me is to leave the back of your card blank. This gives people space to write down notes about where you met or what you talked about, making it easier for them to remember you later – or, worst case, they've got a handy surface for a quick game of tic-tac-toe.

Keep in mind, networking isn't about handing out or collecting as many cards as possible. Share your card with people you genuinely connect with, and treat others' cards with respect. Lastly, always carry a few with you. You never know when an unexpected networking opportunity will pop up, and you'll be ready when it does.

6.5.9 Handling Rejection or Disinterest

Not every networking interaction will lead to a meaningful connection. You'll likely face rejection or disinterest sometimes. When that happens, remember: rejection is rarely personal.

There are many reasons someone might not be open to connecting right then. Maybe they're overwhelmed, distracted, or just not in the mindset to meet new people. It's not about your worth or skills – usually, it's just timing or circumstance. So, don't take it personally.

If someone seems disengaged, politely end the conversation and leave the door open for future opportunities. If you reach out online and get no reply, it's okay to follow up once – but never, ever spam. Overdoing it can hurt your reputation.

Every rejection is a chance to learn and improve. Keep your focus on the bigger picture and move forward. I'll cover dealing with rejection in more depth in Chapter 11.

"The single best thing you can do for your career is keep a good reputation."
– Dylan Mellott

6.5.10 Respecting Boundaries

Everyone has different comfort levels, so pay attention to cues like body language and tone to gauge someone's preferences. Try to keep conversations brief, especially at events, and avoid pushing topics or overstepping time limits if the other person seems disengaged. Respect their personal space, whether it's face-to-face or online.

6.5.11 Following Up

Meeting someone and exchanging contacts is just the first step. What really sets you apart is the follow-up. Sending a thoughtful message after your initial conversation shows you're genuinely interested in maintaining a meaningful connection and not just collecting contacts.

Aim to follow up within 24 to 48 hours. Wait too long, and the conversation fades. Keep it short and personal. Instead of a generic "Nice to meet you," reference something specific from your chat, like a project they're working on or a shared interest. This will show you remember the conversation.

Your goal is to express interest in staying in touch, but without being pushy. Say you'd love to connect, but leave the ball in their court. If they don't reply, don't stress – people get busy. After one or two follow-ups with no response, it's okay to pause. You can always try again later or move on. Like I mentioned before, remember not to spam them.

Follow-ups don't have to be all business. If it's a personal connection, check in with how they're doing or share an update on what you're working on. Over time, the best networking relationships evolve naturally. Just give it the space it needs to grow.

Building a Portfolio

7

In an industry crowded with talented artists, your portfolio is what makes you stand out. It's more than a collection of your best work. It's how studios decide whether you're the right fit for their team. CVs and cover letters are important, but without a strong portfolio, they won't get you through the door, let alone land you the job.

7.1 WHAT TO INCLUDE

When you're up against a sea of skilled artists, your portfolio is your strongest asset. It doesn't need to be massive; it needs to be focused, polished, and relevant. A few well-executed pieces that clearly demonstrate your strengths are far more powerful than a large collection of unfocused or unfinished work.

Your goal isn't to show everything you can do. It's to make it easy for someone to look at your portfolio and think, "This is exactly the artist we need." Sometimes, that just means a few standout pieces. Even two or three strong, polished pieces will do way more for you than ten that look half-baked. Quality beats quantity every time.

Equally important is what you leave out. Don't include work that looks unfinished, rushed, or outdated. Anything half-done or sloppy pulls down the whole portfolio. Each piece should feel complete and intentional. That level of care says a lot about your standards as an artist. Quick studies or experiments are fine if they're clearly labeled as such and you have enough strong, polished pieces to back them up.

Your portfolio should also focus on the role you want. Want to be a character artist? Then, show characters – not environments, VFX, or old school assignments you've outgrown. Keeping unrelated or outdated work in your portfolio can confuse employers and make it harder to see your true strengths.

That doesn't mean you can't show range – you can, but keep it relevant. For example, if you're a prop artist, showing both props and environments can be a strength, as long as everything is polished. Just make sure it all ties back to the kind of roles you're aiming for.

Breakdowns of your work can take your portfolio up a notch. You may include wireframes, texture maps, or animation passes – to name a few – as these demonstrate your process and the technical skills employers look for. Skipping these makes it far more likely for you to be asked to complete an art test (more on art tests in Chapter 9), especially if you're just starting out.

Your portfolio must also be honest and original. If you include a piece you created as part of a team, be clear about your contributions. Specify what you were responsible for – whether it was concepting, modeling, materials, lighting, or animation. This kind of clarity not only builds trust but also helps employers understand how you collaborate and where you add the most value.

And please, never include work that isn't yours. Don't steal someone else's art or rely on AI-generated content. Doing so not only disrespects the community and harms your reputation, but it's also an immediate deal-breaker for employers. Studios want to see your ideas, your execution, and your potential. Show them what *you* can do, and not what an algorithm or someone else made.

Last thing: your portfolio isn't ever "done." As you grow and improve, your portfolio should too. Treat your portfolio as a living document – one that evolves alongside your skills and experience and reflects your continuous development.

> *"Quality over quantity. It sounds obvious, but it's better to have fewer, more impactful pieces."*
>
> – Juan Novelletto
>
> *"The biggest mistake I see in job applications is a portfolio that's too diverse with no clear direction."*
>
> – Etienne Bednarz

7.2 PRESENTING YOUR WORK

Your art could be amazing, but if it's hard to find or not shown off well, people might not stick around long enough to notice your potential. It's not that they don't care – they're usually just busy. Recruiters, leads, and other visitors often skim portfolios fast. So, your top priority? Make a professional portfolio that's easy to navigate.

If your portfolio loads slowly, has broken links, requires many clicks, or isn't mobile-friendly, you're losing people instantly. Your work needs to be easy to access and browse, no matter what device someone's on. Use clean thumbnails, clear titles, and helpful tags, and organize your projects into logical categories. That way, viewers can quickly find what matters and understand what they're looking at without scratching their heads.

Once someone's in, how you present each project matters just as much as the art itself. Even the coolest piece can fall flat if it's not presented well. So take time to polish your renders, frame your shots, and set up your lighting carefully.

Speaking of lighting, this alone can make or break your work. Too dark or blown out? You hide your skills instead of showing them off. Good lighting pulls attention to the details, shapes, and materials and gives your work depth and polish. Think of it like photography: it's not just about creating great art, but about showing it in the best possible light (literally).

Where it makes sense, add brief context to your work. A short caption can go a long way. What was the goal of the project? What tools did you use? And what was your role? This is especially important for collaborative work.

You also want to keep your presentation cohesive overall. That doesn't mean every piece needs to look the same, but your portfolio should have somewhat of a clear rhythm. Wildly different styles, mixed image sizes, or rough screenshots mixed with polished shots make it feel scattered. A bit of variety is good, but just make sure the focus is clear and intentional.

Lead with your strongest, most relevant work. Don't make people dig through several tabs to figure out what you're really good at. As mentioned earlier, recruiters and hiring managers might only spend seconds on your portfolio. Make those seconds count.

If you're uploading your work to platforms like ArtStation, keep in mind that getting seen on the main page can boost your visibility big time. That means your thumbnails need to stand out from the crowd. Here's a tip: take a screenshot of ArtStation's main page, and then swap out one of the thumbnails with your own. Seeing your thumbnail in that context helps you see if it stands out enough among all the others.

If you're unsure how to present your work, take a close look at portfolios from artists in roles you're aiming for. Study how they present their work. Do they include turntables, breakdowns, or wireframes? How clean are their renders? How much context do they give? This gives you a clear benchmark and helps you understand how your own presentation stacks up.

> *"To be considered a professional, you must first look like a professional. Presentation is as important as content."*
>
> – Philippe Routhier

7.3 WHERE TO HOST YOUR PORTFOLIO

Now that you know what to include and how to present your work, let's talk about where to put it. Choosing the right platform is almost as important as the work itself. The platform you choose should suit your goals, style, and audience. In some cases, using more than one platform (e.g., an ArtStation page and a personal website) can give you both visibility and flexibility. Just make sure everything you put online is consistent, polished, and up-to-date.

With that in mind, here's a quick rundown of the most popular platforms game artists use:

- **ArtStation** – Widely considered the industry standard, ArtStation is the go-to platform for game artists. It's used by recruiters, studios, and fellow artists to browse work, discover talent, and stay inspired. It supports high-resolution images, videos, breakdowns, and even blog posts.
  Best for: 2D/3D artists and anyone wanting visibility in the game art community.
- **Personal Website** – Having your own custom website shows initiative and allows for full control over layout, branding, and content. Platforms like Squarespace, Wix, Carrd, and Cargo make it easy to create sleek, mobile-friendly sites without coding. Just be mindful that some of the templates on these platforms can slow down your portfolio, so always test your site thoroughly to ensure it's fast and user-friendly across devices.
  Best for: artists who want to stand out with a personalized portfolio.
- **Behance** – While mainly used in graphic and motion design, Behance can also work for 2D game art and UI/UX portfolios, though it's less common than ArtStation.
  Best for: UI artists, motion designers, or those with a crossover in visual design.
- **GitHub** – If you're a tech artist or tools developer, showcasing your scripts, shaders, or tools on GitHub or a specialized technical portfolio site can be a great complement to your visual work.
  Best for: technical artists or anyone blending code with visuals.
- **Vimeo** – Vimeo is a platform for hosting high-quality, ad-free videos. It's clean, distraction-free and gives you better control over how your content is displayed – including player appearance (logos, colors, and controls), embed behavior, and privacy settings like

password protection. It is ideal for reels or animated pieces where you want things to look sharp and professional.

Best for: animators, cinematic artists, motion designers, or anyone uploading demo reels.

- **YouTube** – YouTube is more informal but incredibly accessible. It's widely used, easy to embed elsewhere (like on ArtStation or personal websites), and great for visibility. Just be aware of ads and suggested content that might distract from your work.

Best for: demo reels, walkthroughs, tutorials, or any other videos you want to share widely. It is also great for building an online presence.

Finding a Job

8

Looking for your first job in the game industry? It's a big deal. It can feel a little intimidating – no doubt about it, but it's also one of the most exciting moments of your career. You're about to turn your passion for art into something real, something that pays the bills and something that pushes you to grow as an artist.

8.1 WHERE AND HOW

Before we jump in, though, it's important to first figure out *where* and *how* you want to work. This is the starting point, and your decision will directly impact the kind of opportunities you seek and how you approach them moving forward.

To get started, ask yourself a few questions: are you open to relocating for a job? Would you be comfortable moving to a new city or even a different country? Do you want to work in an office space, or is the comfort of remote working more your style? Maybe a hybrid setup is the sweet spot, giving you the best of both worlds.

Whatever the case, understanding your own preferences will help you make the right career moves.

8.1.1 Relocating for Work

As you start applying for jobs in the game industry, you'll quickly notice that not all opportunities are in your backyard. In fact, many of them might be in a different city – or even a different country altogether. That means considering relocating often becomes part of the job search.

I've been through that process myself. In 2016, I moved from the Netherlands to the Czech Republic. Leaving home and everything familiar was tough, but it turned out to be one of the best choices I made for both my career and personal growth. Relocation comes with challenges, but it can also open doors you might never access otherwise.

That's especially true as game development jobs tend to cluster in major industry "hotspots" or "hubs." Cities like San Francisco, Los Angeles, Montreal, London, Berlin, Stockholm, and Tokyo are packed with game studios and industry professionals. Living in one of these hubs can give you a serious leg up. More job openings, more studios nearby, and if one studio shuts down or you get laid off, there's usually another opportunity close by. Plus, working alongside some of the best artists around is an amazing way to learn, grow fast, and build valuable connections.

But before you pack your bags, do your research. Look into the cost of living, housing, and transport. Can you afford rent, groceries, and commuting? Just as important, ask yourself if this is a place you'd enjoy living beyond work. Relocating isn't just about the job; it's also a chance to experience a new culture, meet new people, and see the world from a different perspective. At the same time, it can be an emotional challenge – leaving behind family, friends, and routines is never easy, and starting over takes time.

Big cities can also come with hefty price tags. Renting in places like London or San Francisco isn't cheap. Add groceries, transport, and daily expenses, and it can hit your wallet hard. Budget carefully so you're not caught off guard.

If you're moving internationally, visas and work permits can be a headache. It might take weeks or months, and things don't always go smoothly. Some companies help with relocation (visas, housing, and moving costs), so don't hesitate to ask the recruiter about any available support if it's not mentioned.

Of course, relocation isn't for everyone. If the cost or emotional toll feels too high, that's completely valid. There are other ways to build a strong career – remote roles, freelancing, and local studios.

In the end, it's your call. If you're ready for the challenge, relocating can open doors you never imagined. Plan wisely, stay flexible, and embrace the adventure.

8.1.2 Remote Versus Office Work

Another factor to consider is whether you want to work remotely or from an office. The game industry, like many others, has gone through a major shift in recent years. More and more studios are offering remote work opportunities, especially in the wake of the pandemic. But don't get me wrong, traditional office-based roles are still very much a thing. Each of these setups has its own pros and cons, and understanding both sides can help you decide what's best for you.

Let's go over remote work first. Sounds pretty good, right? You get to work from wherever you want. Whether it's your cozy home office, a quiet café, or a secluded cabin in the woods (I'd be down for that) – the location is all up to you. If you're on a budget, remote means you can live somewhere cheaper and still work for a big studio. No need to be stuck in a pricey city just to make a living. One thing to watch out for, though, is that some studios only offer remote roles if you're in the same state, country, or time zone. Always double-check the job listing or ask the recruiter before you get too excited.

Remote work also brings flexibility. Depending on your employment contract, you might be able to set your own working hours, which can be great if you're someone who prefers working in the evenings or early mornings. Even better, you get to set up your workspace exactly how you like it, free from the distractions of a noisy office or the hassle of rush-hour commutes. And, when it's pouring outside, you won't have to worry about getting drenched or dealing with the weather – your office is right at home, cozy and dry.

That said, remote work isn't without its downsides. It can get lonely if you thrive on social interaction. Being at home all day can feel isolating (unless you count your dog or cat as a coworker – great listener, terrible at giving feedback). Communication also tends to be a bit trickier when you're not in the same physical space as your team. Getting feedback can take longer, and you might miss out on those spontaneous team lunches or casual chats by the coffee machine. That physical distance can make it harder to feel connected to the team and the studio's culture.

Now, office work comes with its own wins. Being in the same space means faster, smoother communication. You bounce ideas off each other face-to-face and get feedback instantly without having to wait for a video call or Slack reply. There's something special about working shoulder-to-shoulder with your team – (board) game nights, lunches, and casual hangouts. If that sense of community matters to you, working on-site might be just what you're looking for.

For some of us, having a clear boundary between work and home is important – not just for productivity but for our mental well-being. Working in an office naturally creates that separation; when you leave for the day, you leave work behind. At home, it can be harder to switch off, especially when your workspace is just a few steps from your bed or kitchen table.

If you're just starting out, my best advice is to kick off your career in an office setting. I think it's something everyone should experience at least once if they have the opportunity. You won't truly know what you're missing until you've tried it – and if it turns out not to be your style, remote work is still a great alternative.

I currently work remotely for a studio abroad, but I've spent years working from an office before making the switch. These days, I still get to see my colleagues when visiting company events, and whenever I can, I spend a few extra days working from their office.

Being surrounded by experienced professionals you can turn to for guidance is one of the fastest ways to grow your skills. Not only that, you'll pick up crucial soft skills – like communication, teamwork, and understanding workplace culture and dynamics. As I've mentioned briefly in Chapter 4, these interpersonal skills are harder to develop when you're working solo at home, but they can make a huge impact on your growth.

Ultimately, the decision between remote work and office work really boils down to your personal preferences, career goals, lifestyle, and what the studio offers. Both paths have their perks, and it's about what works best for you.

Not quite ready to pick one? Hybrid setups offer the best of both worlds – splitting time between home and office. Just keep in mind you'll need to live close enough to commute, so relocation might still come into play.

8.1.3 Freelancing

You've probably seen those perfect images of freelancers working from a sunny beach, sipping on a drink while their laptop hums away. For game artists, though, hauling a powerful PC, extra monitors, a graphics tablet, and other gear makes that "beach office" a lot trickier (but not impossible if you're determined).

Freelancing offers freedom, flexibility, and the chance to work with a variety of clients. You choose your projects, set your rates, and work from anywhere. You get to decide what fits your interests and your lifestyle.

That freedom comes with uncertainty. There's no guaranteed paycheck, and steady work means constant effort. Unlike studio jobs, where assignments and paychecks show up regularly, freelancers must actively find clients to keep work flowing.

It's also not just about art skills, either. You need to build yourself a brand, keep your portfolio up-to-date, network, and engage with the community. The more visible you are, the more opportunities come your way.

You're also your own business manager. Handling contracts, setting rates, invoicing, and taxes all fall on you – unless you bring in an accountant to help you out with that. Studio jobs usually handle this for you, but freelancing means these responsibilities fall on your shoulders.

Another important aspect is discipline. Unlike remote studio jobs with set hours, freelancing lets you work whenever you want. But that flexibility can be a trap. Without a routine, it's easy to get derailed by distractions like social media, errands, or household chores. To succeed, you need to establish a routine and manage your time well. It isn't for everyone, and while some thrive in the independence, others struggle with the isolation and lack of structure.

Overall, freelancing is exciting and rewarding for those who value freedom and control. But if you're new to the industry, starting out as a freelancer is extremely tough. Without prior experience, a few titles under your belt, and a strong network, landing gigs can be incredibly challenging.

8.2 WHERE TO FIND JOBS

When you're ready to start your job search, the first step is knowing where to look. But before we continue, I want to highlight that not all job opportunities are publicly advertised. Many studios get flooded with applications, and some roles are filled through internal referrals before they even hit the job boards. That's why networking is so important. It helps you hear about openings that haven't been widely shared (yet).

That said, plenty of opportunities are still online, so don't worry. Most companies post openings on their own websites first, so regularly check the career pages of studios you're interested in. You'll also find listings on game art forums like Polycount and social platforms such as LinkedIn, Discord, X, Bluesky, and Facebook.

Reddit is another place you could check out, particularly for indie developers posting jobs or looking for collaborators. Just know that studios usually post on their official sites or through professional job boards instead of Reddit.

Below, I've gathered a few platforms to help you in your search:

- **8bitplay** (https://8bitplay.com/jobs/)
- **80.lv** (https://80.lv/jobs)
- **ArtStation** (https://www.artstation.com/jobs/)
- **CreativeHeads.net** (https://www.creativeheads.net/)
- **GameCompanies.com** (https://gamecompanies.com/)
- **GameDevMap** (https://www.gamedevmap.com/)
- **GameJobs.Co** (https://gamejobs.co/)
- **GameJobs.work** (https://gamejobs.work/)
- **GamesIndustry.biz** (https://jobs.gamesindustry.biz/)
- **Games Jobs Direct** (https://www.gamesjobsdirect.com/art-jobs)
- **Games Jobs Live** (https://gamesjobslive.niceboard.co/)
- **Glassdoor** (https://www.glassdoor.com/Job/index.htm)
- **Hitmarker** (https://hitmarker.net/jobs)
- **Indeed** (https://www.indeed.com/)

- **InGame Job** (https://ingamejob.com/en/jobs)
- **LinkedIn** (https://www.linkedin.com/jobs/)
- **Outscal** (https://outscal.io/jobs)
- **Polycount** (https://polycount.com/forum)
- **Reddit** (r/GameDevClassifieds, r/gamedev, r/forhire)
- **RemoteGameJobs.com** (https://remotegamejobs.com/)
- **UK Games Map** (http://map.gamesmap.uk/)
- **Work With Indies** (https://www.workwithindies.com/)

8.3 UNDERSTANDING JOB LISTINGS

Job listings can sometimes feel vague or overwhelming, especially if you're just starting out. You might read one and think, "What does this mean?" Learning how to break them down helps you figure out if the role's right for you and how to make your application stand out.

Most listings follow a familiar structure: job title, responsibilities, required skills, and "nice-to-haves." But job titles alone don't always tell the full story. Sometimes, they don't reflect the actual scope of the role, so make sure to read the full description before deciding to apply.

If a listing feels unclear or leaves you with questions, don't hesitate to reach out to the recruiter or hiring manager. It shows initiative and helps you get a clearer picture of what they are looking for.

Responsibilities tell you what you'll be doing day-to-day, while required skills outline what you *must* know. "Nice-to-haves" are bonus skills that can help you stand out but aren't mandatory.

You'll also notice terms like "permanent," "contract," or "hybrid." A permanent role usually includes benefits and long-term employment. Contract roles tend to be short-term or project-based. "Hybrid" means a mix of remote and in-office work, so be sure to check location requirements and whether the company offers any flexibility.

Watch for keywords that signal experience level. "Junior" or "entry-level" means the role is geared toward beginners, while "mid-level" or "senior" requires more experience. As discussed in Chapter 2, mid-level roles don't include a prefix – so a title like "Concept Artist," for example, is typically aimed at mid-level candidates.

You'll sometimes see listings asking for things like "1–2 years of experience" for a junior role, which can feel impossible if you haven't had a first job yet. In creative fields like game art, a solid portfolio often matters more than years of experience. If your work is strong and relevant, it's still worth applying.

And if you don't tick every box, that's okay. It's rare to meet *every* qualification. If you tick more than half, you're likely a strong candidate. The "nice-to-have" skills can also help fill in any gaps.

"Apply anyway. All you need is one yes."

– Shona Markusen

Now let's look at a sample job listing for a junior 2D artist position. This example is based on real-world listings and should give you a clear idea of what to expect and how to approach it:

Junior 2D Artist[1]

Studio: Pocket Mentor Interactive[2]
Location: On-Site or Remote (EU Time Zones Preferred)[3]
Job Type: Contract or Full-Time[4]
Salary Range: €30,000 – €45,000/year[5]

About the Role[6]:

We're looking for a passionate junior 2D artist to join our growing mobile games team. If you love creating colorful, fantasy-driven art and want to grow in a supportive environment, this is the role for you!

Responsibilities[7]:

- Design and illustrate 2D characters, environments, and UI assets.
- Collaborate with designers and producers to deliver assets on schedule.
- Implement feedback quickly and professionally.
- Maintain consistency in visual style.

Requirements[8]:

- Portfolio showcasing stylized 2D art.
- Proficiency in Photoshop, Illustrator, or similar tools.
- Understanding of color, lighting, and shape language.
- Previous game development experience with at least one shipped title.

Nice-to-Have[9]:

- Experience with Unity or familiarity with animation tools (Spine, After Effects).

Notes:

[1] The "junior" title indicates an entry-level position. These are usually focused on learning and growth, and you can expect mentorship and collaborative teamwork to help you develop your skills.

[2] Knowing the studio can help you research their past projects, team size, and work culture. Always check their website and socials to learn more before applying.

[3] This suggests flexibility, but they prefer someone who can work within European time zones. Even if you're remote, being within a few hours of their schedule is likely important for collaboration.

[4] This means they're open to different kinds of working arrangements. A contract role may be short-term with less stability, while full-time usually includes benefits and long-term potential.

[5] Compensation may depend on your location and experience, so use the listed range as a general guideline.

[6] The brief role description summarizes the main focus and expectations of the position.

[7] The responsibilities outline your typical day-to-day tasks and help you understand what skills to highlight in your portfolio and interviews.

[8] The listed requirements are the minimum qualifications needed. If you meet most of these and have a strong portfolio, you're in a competitive position to apply.

[9] "Nice-to-have" skills are not mandatory but can set you apart from other applicants.

8.4 TALENT ACQUISITION

If you're wondering who's behind the scenes hiring at game studios, it's usually the talent acquisition team, which is part of the HR or People Operations department. This team is responsible for the entire hiring process – from sourcing candidates and coordinating interviews to onboarding new hires and promoting the studio as a great place to work. If you're applying directly through a game studio's website, it's usually the talent acquisition team – including recruiters – with whom you'll be in contact.

Recruiters play a central role in the hiring process. They actively search for talent and may reach out to you directly if they find your profile appealing. While recruiters might not always be focused on junior roles, sharing your work online can significantly increase the likelihood of being contacted by one.

8.5 RECRUITMENT AGENCIES

Recruitment agencies serve a similar purpose as talent acquisition – helping to hire talent – but are external firms hired by game studios to help them find candidates for specific roles. They operate outside of the studio and often specialize in finding talent for hard-to-recruit positions like seniors, leads, art directors, or specific niche skills. They actively scout on socials, looking for talent that matches their criteria.

In my experience, once I moved into a more senior role, messages from recruitment agencies headhunting for talent started coming in much more frequently. These agencies typically work on a project basis, stepping in when a studio needs to fill positions quickly or find candidates for niche roles.

Applying for a Job

9

You found a job you're interested in, so the next logical step is to apply. But hold up just a sec. Before you hit send on that application, there are a few things you need to know and have ready. Getting these right will give you a way better shot at landing the interview.

9.1 CV (RÉSUMÉ)

A curriculum vitae (CV), also known as a résumé, is a document summarizing your professional experience, education, skills, and accomplishments. When applying for jobs, your CV is often the second impression you make on a hiring manager – after your portfolio, of course. In many game art roles, the portfolio does most of the heavy lifting, but a clear and professional CV can support your application and make it easier for studios to understand your experience and background.

Here's a clear and practical structure to help you build a solid CV (also illustrated in Figure 9.1):

- **Header**: The header is the first thing a hiring manager will see, so make sure it's clear and easy to read. Put your name at the top (so they know who you are), followed by your job title (so they know what you do). Your job title should reflect your role or professional focus (think "Character Artist," "Environment Artist," "Animator," etc.). Avoid vague titles like "Aspiring Artist" – they only weaken your position.
- **Contact Details**: Include your email, phone number, location, and a link to your portfolio and/or socials, either within the header or as a separate section. Double-check that your URLs work. It's also enough to list just your city and country; a full street address isn't necessary. Use a professional email address that includes your real

DOI: 10.1201/9781003492320-9

John Doe
Environment Artist

john.doe@example.com   +123-456-7890

Los Angeles, California   **example.com**
linkedin.com

Summary

Creative, detail-oriented Environment Artist with a strong foundation in 3D modeling, texturing, and world-building. Proficient in industry-standard tools such as Maya, Blender, Substance Painter, and Unreal Engine 5. Experienced in creating assets for both mobile and console games, driven by a passion for storytelling through immersive environments.

Work Experience

January 2026 - present

Freelance Environment Artist (Part-time)
[Company Name] - Remote

- Designed and built small game-ready scenes for clients
- Delivered clean topology and PBR textures optimized for real-time engines

July 2024 - January 2026

3D Environment Artist Intern
[Company Name] - Los Angeles, CA

- Modeled and textured modular environment assets for a stylized platformer
- Collaborated with a small team to optimize assets for performance in Unreal

Achievements

ArtStation Staff Pick
Environment project "Forgotten Sanctum" selected as a Staff Pick and widely shared in the digital art community.

Featured in 80 Level
Interviewed about workflow tips and design philosophy for stylized environment creation using Unreal Engine 5.

Education

2020 - 2024

University of Game Artists, Los Angeles
Bachelor Degree in Game Art & Design

Software

Maya - Intermediate

Blender - Expert

Substance Painter - Expert

Photoshop - Expert

Unreal Engine 5 - Novice

SpeedTree - Beginner

Expertise

PBR, modular asset creation, asset optimization and integration, scandata cleanup

Languages

English - Native

Spanish - Fluent

French - Conversational

FIGURE 9.1 Sample CV illustrating the structure outlined in the text.

name (e.g., john.doe@example.com), and avoid informal or quirky addresses (looking at you, "NoobSlayer99@example.com").

- **Summary** (optional): This section is optional, but it can be a powerful addition to your CV. Think of it as your elevator pitch: a brief one-to-three-sentence summary at the top of your CV that highlights your experience, skills, and the value you bring to the company. The goal is to give employers a quick snapshot of your expertise and what sets you apart. For example: "Creative, detail-oriented 3D Character Artist with 4+ years of experience creating assets for mobile and console games with a passion for stylized characters."

- **Work Experience**: List relevant roles in reverse-chronological order, with your most recent job listed first. Include job title, company, and dates of employment. More importantly, use bullet points to highlight *what you achieved*, not just what you did. For instance, instead of saying, "Worked as a Concept Artist," try something like, "Designed a custom player skin concept that became a community favorite for a mobile game."

- **Achievements** (optional): Use this section to showcase standout accomplishments that highlight your skills, recognition, or contributions to the industry. This could include creating game mods, participating in game jams, ArtStation Staff Picks, competition wins (e.g., Game Jam awards), or features on websites like 80 Level and The Rookies. If you don't yet have much studio experience, achievements can fill that gap with proof of quality and initiative.

  For example:

  - Produced a YouTube series on creating facial animation for interactive dialogue scenes, reaching over 10,000 viewers.
  - Given a talk on "Creating Realistic Environments for Games" at GDC 2024.
  - Interviewed by 80 Level about character art techniques.

- **Education**: List your levels of education, such as a degree, diploma, or certification, and include the name of the institution and your graduation year. You can list more than one, but if you've got many certifications or degrees, focus on the most relevant or recent ones. And if your education doesn't align perfectly with the job, don't worry. Highlight any coursework, special projects, or extracurriculars that tie in with the skills needed for the role. For example, if you completed a certification from an accredited online course, make sure to mention it.

- **Skills**: Focus this section on your software proficiencies and specialized expertise (hard skills), since soft skills are usually assessed through the interview rather than listed outright.

  I recommend splitting this section into two clear parts: *Software* and *Expertise*. This separation helps hiring managers to quickly identify your knowledge of software and specialized skills.

For example:

- **Software**: List the software programs you're familiar with, such as Blender, Maya, Unity, Unreal Engine, ZBrush, Photoshop, and any other relevant tools.
- **Expertise**: Highlight your specialized skills, such as asset integration, scan data cleanup, character skinning, real-time hair creation, and hard surface sculpting.

- **Languages Spoken**: List your native language first, then add any others you speak, along with your proficiency level (e.g., native, fluent, and conversational). This gives employers a clear picture of your communication skills across languages.

9.1.1 Additional CV Considerations

Ideally, your CV should fit on a single page – especially if you're just starting out. While it may seem tempting to stretch it to two pages, this can often lead to unnecessary fluff. That said, if you're an experienced artist with several titles under your belt, having two pages is acceptable. But in any case, less is more.

Stick to a clean, text-based layout that's easy to scan. Use bullet points, bold headings, enough white space, and columns for neat organization. Try to avoid overly decorative templates, flashy graphs, or unconventional formatting. The goal is clarity. Hiring managers typically skim CVs quickly, so your information must be easy to read without visual clutter.

Including a photo on your CV isn't necessary. Studios will likely look you up online anyway, especially if you include URLs to your portfolio or socials – so if they want to see who you are, they can.

When it comes to listing your skills, avoid vague self-assessments such as skill bars, graphs, or percentage ratings (e.g., "Photoshop: 90%"; see Figure 9.2). They might look sleek, but they often do more harm than good. They take up valuable space, can be misinterpreted, and are frequently unreadable by applicant tracking systems (ATS), which we'll cover later. Instead, be honest and use clear proficiency levels like "Beginner," "Competent," "Advanced," or "Expert." You can see how these levels are applied in the sample CV shown in Figure 9.1.

Hobbies? It is usually best to leave them off your CV. Focus on skills and experience instead. If a hobby directly connects to the role you're applying for, you can mention it briefly in your cover letter to show how it relates. Just keep them relevant and concise.

Blender	100%
ZBrush	90%
Photoshop	70%
Substance Painter	50%
Unreal Engine	80%
Marmoset Toolbag	60%

Blender	⦿ ⦿ ⦿ ⦿ ⦿
ZBrush	⦿ ⦿ ⦿ ⦿ ⦿
Photoshop	⦿ ⦿ ⦿ ⦿ ○
Substance Painter	⦿ ⦿ ⦿ ○ ○
Unreal Engine	⦿ ⦿ ⦿ ⦿ ○
Marmoset Toolbag	⦿ ⦿ ⦿ ○ ○

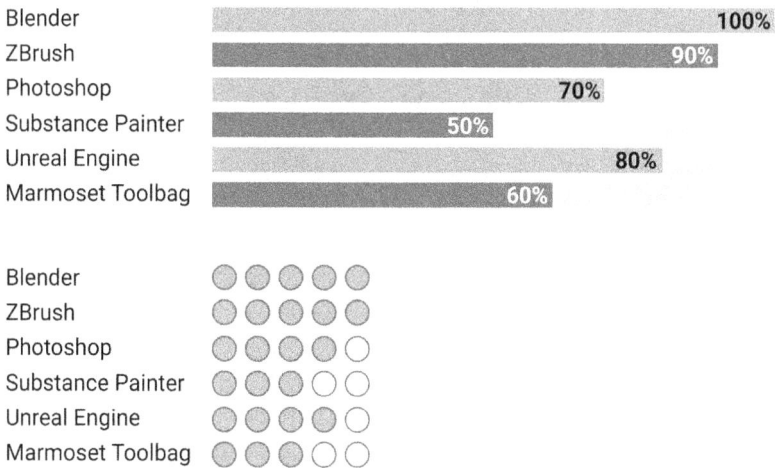

FIGURE 9.2   Examples of visual skill ratings that are best avoided on a CV.

Some people also like to add "References available on request" or list contacts at the bottom of their CV. Honestly, that's not necessary. Most companies don't bother checking references until much later in the process – if at all – and that line just takes up valuable space. If you have strong references, you can always mention them in your cover letter or bring them up during an interview.

Once you're happy with your CV, export it as a PDF. It's easy for anyone to open and protects your work from being accidentally changed. The same goes for your cover letter, which we'll get to next.

Last but definitely not least, proofread. Even if you've skimmed it a hundred times, mistakes can sneak in. Get a colleague, friend, or mentor to take a look. Fresh eyes catch what you might miss and can offer solid feedback to polish things up. Fingers crossed you won't spot any typos in this book after I said that . . . but if you do, well, let's just pretend they were intentional.

9.2 COVER LETTER

For many, writing a cover letter is one of the most dreaded parts of the whole application process. While it may not be the most exciting task, it can be an important factor for you to land that interview. A well-crafted cover letter gives you the opportunity to introduce yourself beyond your portfolio and CV, showcasing your passion, personality, and fit for the role.

The best cover letters don't just repeat what's already on your CV. They explain *why* you're interested, how your skills fit, and what makes you a great match for the team.

Your cover letter should be concise, ideally one page, and with a clear structure. That's all you need. No walls of text, no fluff. Just four or five paragraphs that get straight to the point. Here's a simple outline to guide you:

1. **Introduction (one paragraph)**

   - If you're applying through a studio's website or general email, you can address your letter as "Dear [Studio Name]." Even better, if you've connected with a recruiter through networking, contact them directly and use their name instead. Just make sure your application actually lands in *their* inbox.
   - Clearly mention the job title and company name you're applying for.
   - Briefly introduce yourself and your background.
   - Show enthusiasm for the role and the company. Make it clear why this opportunity excites you.
   - If someone at the company referred you or you have a connection within the studio, mention them here – but only if they've given you permission to do so. Why? It's respectful, they might be contacted, and it could even lead to them advocating for you internally.

2. **Main Body (two to three paragraphs)**

   - Reference the studio's work. Show you're familiar with what they do, and highlight the projects that resonate with you.
   - Showcase how your skills and experience align with the company's needs. This is where you get to talk about how you're a great fit for the role.
   - Emphasize the skills that are most relevant to the job and make it clear how you bring value.
   - Back it up with concrete examples of past projects to show what you're capable of.
   - As mentioned earlier, hobbies usually don't belong on your CV. But if they tie directly to the role, you may mention them briefly here to show their relevance.
   - If you've had career breaks or job shifts, it's okay to mention them here – only if you want to, though. There is no need to go in-depth either.

3. **Conclusion (one paragraph)**

• Wrap it up by reiterating how excited you are about the role.
• Let them know you're available for further discussion.
• Mention that your portfolio and CV are attached, so the recruiter has all the relevant info at their fingertips.
• Sign off with your name at the bottom, followed by your portfolio link.

Now, let's cover a few common mistakes. As with your CV, proofread. Read it carefully, then read it again. Typos and grammar mistakes are an easy way to get skipped over. Better yet, have someone else read it, too. Avoid overused phrases like "I'm passionate about games." Everyone is. Be specific about *why* you're passionate about *their* games.

And please, don't copy and paste the same letter everywhere. I've seen people (and, I'll admit, I've made this mistake myself) accidentally mention the wrong studio. Trust me, that's not a good look and hard to recover from. Hiring managers can tell who took the time to get to know the company and who just swapped out names in a template.

Finally, make sure your portfolio URL is correct, opens without issues, and doesn't require any login or download. Avoid using Google Drive or cloud storage platforms that ask recruiters to sign in or download a zip file. Your portfolio should be instantly accessible, clean, and easy to navigate. Make it as frictionless as possible for them to see your work.

Will every recruiter read your cover letter? No. But when they do, it can make all the difference. It shows that you're not just looking for *any* job, but that you want *this* job. And you'd be surprised at how much the process of writing one can help you clarify your goals and motivations, making you more confident and prepared for the potential interview.

So, take those extra few minutes. Personalize it. Make it count. It's a small effort that might just open the door to your next opportunity.

9.3 KEYWORDS AND ATS

Larger and some mid-sized studios don't always look at your CV at first. They sometimes use applicant tracking systems (ATS) to filter through tons of applications. These systems scan for keywords that match the job description, and if your CV is missing the right ones, it might get skipped over entirely.

It's hard to tell if a company uses ATS, so your best bet is to always tweak your CV to get past the system. How? By tailoring it to the job.

Take a good look at the job listing and pick out important words about skills, tools, and experience. If they want someone who knows Unreal Engine, Maya, or ZBrush, make sure those terms show up in your resume – assuming you actually know your way around them.

Also, pull keywords from the job's responsibilities and qualifications. But don't go crazy stuffing your CV with keywords just for the sake of it. You still want to sound like a real person.

Remember, passing the ATS is just the first step. After that, a real person reads your CV, so make sure it's clear, honest, and stands out. The goal is to balance robot-proofing with genuine personality.

9.4 LEVERAGING REFERRALS

In a highly competitive field, having someone inside the company or industry put in a good word for you can seriously boost your chances of landing an interview. A referral helps you stand out, gives you instant credibility, and makes hiring managers feel more confident about you. Companies love referrals because they lower the risk of a bad hire. Simply put, who you know can be just as important as what you know.

Here's where your network starts to work for you. The more genuine connections you have, the better the odds someone will think of you when a role opens up. Plus, many studios even reward employees who refer great candidates who get hired.

So, if you know someone at a company, don't be shy about asking for a referral. It's not a guaranteed ticket in, but it definitely works in your favor. Use that to your advantage whenever you can.

9.5 ART TESTS

Art tests are a common part of the hiring process for game art roles. With tons of candidates competing, studios need a way to dig deeper than just portfolios and CVs. These tests let them see your skills, how you handle deadlines, and how you work under pressure. Sure, it can feel like an extra hurdle, but it's also your chance to show what you're really made of.

For junior artists, an art test might be the only way to prove your potential, especially if you don't have much professional experience yet. Mid-level or senior artists might get tested, too, but it's less common if you've got shipped games under your belt and a strong portfolio.

Usually, the test involves creating an asset under a tight deadline with specific guidelines. Some briefs are strict; some leave room for interpretation – whatever it is, read everything carefully. If you're unclear about anything, ask the recruiter or hiring manager. Double-check deadlines, plan your time well, and if you need an extension, be honest and ask early. Blowing the deadline is one of the quickest ways to hurt your chances.

If the test requires matching the studio's style, take some time to research their work. Check out the artists on their team to get a feel for the quality and style they expect. This will help you deliver something that aligns with their expectations.

Most art tests aren't paid (99% of them, give or take). It's a controversial topic – many artists (rightfully) view them as free labor, especially when studios request fully polished assets that could be used in production. Still, it's worth asking if you can include the work in your portfolio. That way, even if you don't get the job, you still walk away with something useful.

> *"Research the studio where you'd like to work and create pieces that match their style and quality. This will give them confidence that you can work there! "*
> – Juan Novelletto

The Interview 10

The interview is your chance to turn your application into an actual job. It's more than just answering questions. It's where you get to show who you are, what you're capable of, and why you're the right fit for the job.

10.1 TYPES OF INTERVIEWS

Job interviews typically fall into three categories: in-person, virtual, and informal. Each has its own set of expectations, challenges, and advantages. Let's take a quick look at each type so you're prepared for any situation.

10.1.1 In-Person Interviews

In-person interviews give you a chance to connect with the team more personally and see the company environment up close. Some studios – especially those abroad – might even cover your travel and accommodation if they're seriously interested. However, this is more commonly offered for senior or highly specialized roles.

As with any interview, preparation is key. Plan your route in advance to avoid being late or stuck in traffic. Aim to arrive slightly early – not too early, just enough to show that you're punctual and reliable.

If it's your first visit to the studio, you'll likely get a tour. This is your chance to observe everything – the office setup and team vibe – and get a feel for the culture. Could you see yourself thriving here?

When meeting team members, be sure to engage respectfully. Everyone you meet – from the receptionist to the interviewers – is forming an impression, so be polite and professional throughout. First impressions matter.

10.1.2 Virtual Interviews

Virtual interviews have become a staple in hiring, especially in the game industry, where companies work with talent worldwide. Whether it's for a remote role or logistical reasons, a virtual interview can be just as impactful as an in-person one.

If you've been scheduled for a virtual interview, it's a good time to check your tech. Make sure your Internet is stable, your camera and mic work, and your interview platform (Zoom, Teams, etc.) is ready. Nothing's worse than last-minute tech issues, so get everything running smoothly ahead of time.

Next, think about your location. Find a quiet, well-lit spot with a clean background where you won't be distracted. If your background isn't ideal, don't worry – most platforms have virtual backgrounds to blur what's behind you. Just ensure the lighting's on your face, not behind you, so you're clearly visible on camera.

And if something doesn't go as planned – whether a technical hiccup or miscommunication – don't sweat it. Stay calm, politely acknowledge the issue, and handle it. If anything's unclear, ask for clarification.

10.1.3 Informal Interviews

Unlike scheduled interviews, informal interviews can happen anywhere unexpectedly – on a train, at a café, during a meetup, or in the middle of a conference. You might not even realize it's an "interview" until it's over.

They are great for showing the real you. That said, professionalism still matters. What you say shapes how people see you, so be intentional with your words.

You don't need a rehearsed pitch, but having a few talking points about your work ready can help. Ask about their projects or experience (while respecting NDAs), and listen closely. Learning about the person and their company not only shows you care but also gives insight into their culture and what they're looking for in candidates.

Even if it doesn't lead straight to a job, it's still a valuable opportunity to grow your network. Don't hesitate to ask to connect on LinkedIn or swap contact info. Keeping a business card handy for situations like these is never a bad idea.

10.2 INTERVIEW PREPARATIONS

Now that you've got a sense of the types of interviews you might face, it's time to start preparing for them. (Well, maybe not the informal ones – you can't fully prepare for those, and that's kind of the point.) But when it comes to the more structured interviews, preparation goes beyond just practicing how to talk about your work experience clearly – though that's definitely important too. To really stand out, you need to put in some extra effort.

10.2.1 Research the Company

First, research the company you're interviewing with. I'm not talking about just skimming their website or checking out their latest game. You need to understand who they are. What do they stand for? What games are they known for? What are their lesser-known titles? How many employees do they have? You want to revisit their job posting too, so you can tailor your answers to what they're looking for. This is your chance to show that you're not only a fit for the role but also for their team and culture.

You've probably already done this – but if not, play their games. If that's not possible, watch gameplay videos or walkthroughs. It's not required, but bringing up their games in conversation shows effort and gives you easy talking points – plus, it helps you figure out if you'd actually enjoy working there. That said, avoid criticizing their work unless you're specifically asked to give feedback – and even then, keep it constructive and professional without tearing them down. Negative comments can easily be taken the wrong way and hurt your chances.

If you want to go the extra mile, look for behind-the-scenes content, interviews, or blog posts. These often reveal insights into their creative process and culture that aren't usually on the front page.

Sometimes, hiring managers will provide you with the names of the people who'll be interviewing you. If they don't, it's perfectly fine to ask for that information. This gives you a chance to look into their backgrounds – see their work, how long they've been with the company, and their experience in the industry. Knowing who you'll meet also helps you feel prepared and confident when introductions happen.

The goal is to be informed enough to ask thoughtful questions about the role or the team's work – not about the interviewer personally, and not in a way that makes you seem like you're stalking. Keep it professional and avoid delving into their personal lives. That means steering clear of connecting on personal social platforms like Facebook before the interview. LinkedIn is generally fine, but it depends on the individual. If you aren't connected yet, it's safest to wait until after the interview to send a LinkedIn connection request, once some rapport has been built. And of course, if you land the job and get to know them better, connecting on more personal platforms (like Facebook) may feel more appropriate over time.

Remember, they'll likely look you up, too. So, take a moment to review what's out there on the Internet with your name on it, and clean up anything that could work against you.

Doing your research isn't just about impressing them. It shows you're genuinely passionate about the role and the studio. You're not just applying for any job; you're specifically interested in working with them. That distinction can set you apart from other applicants and show you're truly invested in the opportunity.

10.2.2 Prepare Answers

During the interview, you're going to be asked questions. Some will be straight-forward. Others? Not so much. That's part of the process. Interviewers aren't just evaluating your skills; they want to see how you think on your feet. You might get some questions that throw you off guard (as they're often meant to do), and that's okay. What matters most is how you respond. If you don't know the answer, don't bluff. Never feel like you have to make something up. Trust me, interviewers can spot a lie from a mile away. The best thing you can do is be honest. Admitting that you don't know something is actually something interviewers appreciate more than a half-baked answer.

> *"Broad, open-ended questions have been the most challenging I've faced in interviews."*
>
> – Quinn Bogaerts

To help you prep, I've put together a list of questions you might run into. If you've got an interview coming up, take a few minutes and try answering these out loud:

• Can you tell us a bit about yourself?
• Can you walk us through your CV?
• What got you interested in game art?
• Who or what inspires your work?
• What are your hobbies or interests outside of work?
• What's your favorite game, and why?
• What accomplishment are you most proud of?
• Where do you see yourself in five years?
• What do you know about our studio and the games we make?
• Why do you want to work here?

- What makes you a good fit for our team?
- Why did you leave your last position (or why are you looking to leave)?
- Walk us through your portfolio. Which piece means the most to you, and why? Which piece is your weakest, and how would you improve it?
- How do you prioritize your tasks during a busy day?
- How do you handle feedback and criticism?
- Tell us about a time you had a tight deadline. How'd you get through it?
- Ever had a disagreement on a team? How did you handle it?
- If you get a task with little to no direction, how do you tackle it?
- Say the art style changes halfway through a project – how would you adapt?
- How do you stay up-to-date with industry trends and new tools?
- Can you describe a project where you had to learn something new quickly?
- How do you balance creativity with technical constraints?

Along with those, expect some technical questions too. These are meant to see how you solve problems and how well you understand the work itself. Of course, what you get asked will depend on the role you're being interviewed for – as well as the studio, team, project, and many other factors. For example:

- Which software and tools do you use most in your workflow?
- What's your workflow for creating a game-ready asset from start to finish?
- If we asked you to model a stylized treasure chest (this could be anything depending on your role), how would you approach it from start to finish?
- How do you optimize 3D assets for performance without losing quality?
- What's your approach to texturing, and how do you keep consistency across assets?
- Can you explain the physically based rendering (PBR) workflow?
- What are common challenges in baking texture maps, and how do you solve them?
- How do you handle topology for models that need to be animated?
- Can you explain what a normal map is?
- What are some of the biggest technical limits you've had to work around?

10.2.3 Prepare Questions

Now, let's talk about the questions *you* bring to the table.

This step often gets overlooked, but really – it's way more important than most people think. It's your chance to show interest and get the info you need to decide if the job and company are a good match for you, too.

Remember, interviews aren't just about impressing them. You're evaluating the company as much as they're evaluating you. And since you'll potentially spend a good chunk of your life working there, it's worth making sure it's a place you actually want to be.

A quick tip: skip the questions you can easily find on their website. Instead, dig a little deeper. Ask thoughtful, specific questions that show you've done your homework and that you're serious about the role.

For example, you might ask about the challenges they're currently facing in their art pipeline, the tools they use in production, or how artists collaborate with other teams. It's also worth asking about career development, how feedback is shared, and the direction of upcoming projects.

When you ask questions like these, you're proving you're not just ticking boxes. You're showing you're genuinely interested and mentally already part of the team.

To get you started, here are some questions you could bring to your next interview:

- How does the art team collaborate with design, programming, and other departments?
- What are some challenges the art team is dealing with in the pipeline?
- Which tools and software does the team mainly use?
- What's the feedback process like during development?
- How do you keep the art style consistent across a diverse team?
- What are the expectations around deadlines and balancing quality with speed?
- How does the team stay motivated during long production cycles or tough roadblocks?
- How does the studio support continuous learning and skill development?
- What's the team culture like? How do you build camaraderie and keep communication open?
- How do remote or hybrid work setups impact collaboration?
- Can you share any upcoming projects or technologies the art team is excited about?
- What is your approach toward overtime?

- What's the balance between creative freedom and sticking to the established art direction?
- How involved is the art team in early concept and design phases?
- How does the company support work–life balance for its employees?
- What are the company's core values?
- How does the studio approach diversity and inclusion?
- What kind of social or team-building activities do you have?
- How do you support employees' well-being?
- And my personal favorite: what do *you* enjoy most about working here?

10.2.4 Mock Interviews

Feeling nervous before a big interview? That's completely normal. It just means the opportunity matters to you. The truth is, you're not alone. You'd be surprised how many people, even seasoned professionals, feel nervous before an interview. The good news? Practice really does help.

Run through your answers with someone you trust. Record yourself. Say your answers out loud in front of a mirror. Whatever works for you. I still remember prepping for one of my first interviews for an internship – nervous as anything. I ended up doing mock interviews with my university English teacher (thank you, Anita!), and her feedback helped me feel a lot more confident going in.

Mock interviews aren't about memorizing perfect answers. They help you get used to talking about your work under pressure. And once that feels familiar, the nerves calm down. The more you do it, the easier it becomes.

10.3 NDAS

Confidentiality is a big deal in the game industry – and non-disclosure agreements (NDAs) are pretty much standard in the hiring process. Why? Because studios need to protect their ideas, keep things under wraps, and avoid unnecessary pressure before they're ready to go public.

If you're interviewing, chances are you'll come across an NDA pretty early on, especially before seeing games still in development. Basically, these agreements say, "What happens behind closed doors stays behind closed doors." By signing, you promise not to share anything about the projects, company secrets, or anything that's not public knowledge.

Pay close attention to how long the NDA lasts. Some are short term; others can stick around for years. And breaking one? That's a serious no-no. It can cost you your job, lead to fines or legal trouble, and even hurt your chances at other companies (word travels fast).

So, take your time reading it through, and don't hesitate to ask questions if anything's unclear. Most of the time, NDAs aren't something to stress about, as long as you're careful and follow the rules.

10.4 MASTERING THE INTERVIEW

An interview isn't just about answering questions. It's your chance to show who you really are, what you can do, and why you're the perfect fit for the job. Think of this as your moment to turn your application into an actual job offer. Many of the principles we covered in Chapter 6, *Networking and Events* – such as being yourself, overcoming anxiety, and communicating effectively – also apply here.

10.4.1 Be Yourself

We've already covered how important it is to be yourself, but it's worth repeating because it matters just as much in interviews.

It's tempting to put on an idealized version of yourself, especially when you're really hoping to land the job. But let me tell you, authenticity speaks louder than a rehearsed, polished persona. People can tell when you're not being genuine, and that's not the impression you want to leave.

Instead, be honest and confident in who you are, but also stay humble. There's a big difference between confidence and ego. Confidence is about knowing your value and being able to communicate it clearly. Ego, on the other hand, comes off as arrogant – like you think you've got nothing left to learn. That can be a huge red flag for employers. No one wants to work with someone who can't take feedback, collaborate, or admit when they don't know something.

10.4.2 Be on Time

Being on time is one of the simplest ways to make a good first impression and shows you respect the interviewer's time. Arriving late can leave you stressed and may make you seem unreliable or disorganized.

Before your interview, double-check the time, date, and location – virtual or in-person. Aim to arrive 10–15 minutes early to handle surprises and settle in.

As mentioned before, don't wait until the last minute to test your setup for virtual interviews. Double-check that your Internet is stable, your camera and mic are working, and your interview platform (like Zoom or Teams) is fully ready.

You could also set reminders on your phone or calendar to not lose track of time, but don't forget to put your phone on "Do Not Disturb" or turn it off completely before the interview starts. Nothing kills the flow faster than an unexpected notification buzzing in the middle of your conversation.

If you find yourself running late for any reason, be sure to let them know as soon as possible. The same applies to virtual interviews; if you run into any last-minute tech issues, keep them in the loop, and they'll appreciate the heads-up.

10.4.3 Body Language

We touched on body language back in Chapter 6, when we talked about things like posture, eye contact, and open gestures, and how they affect the way you come across. But in interviews? These nonverbal signals carry even more weight.

How you sit, stand, and move says a lot before you even say a word. So, keep your posture solid, make eye contact, and bring some good energy. Show that you're engaged and ready.

On the flip side, if you're fidgeting or looking disconnected, it can come off as nervous or uninterested. That's the last thing you want.

10.4.4 Taking Feedback

If they give you notes on your portfolio during the interview, don't get defensive. Take it in with grace. See it as a chance to get better. And if you've done an art test, chances are they'll ask about it here too, so be ready to walk them through your process.

Doing this doesn't just prove you're open to learning. It tells them you're adaptable, you play well with others, and you're serious about growing. Being upfront about your strengths and weaknesses is the kind of attitude that makes you stand out.

> *"What makes a candidate stand out from the rest in the hiring process is clear communication and a proactive approach to learning, especially through experimentation and learning from failure."*
>
> – Mohsen Tabasi

10.4.5 Presenting Your Work

Even if they've already seen your portfolio, be ready to walk the interviewer through it. Don't assume they'll remember every detail or won't want the story behind each piece. They might pull up your work on their screen, but it's smart to bring your own laptop or tablet just in case. Not sure if that's needed? Ask the recruiter ahead of time.

In virtual interviews, they may share their screen or ask you to share yours. Either way, be prepared. Organize your files beforehand; open the pieces you want to show, clean up your desktop, and close any distracting tabs. A cluttered desktop can come off as disorganized, but a clean one shows you're focused, prepared, and professional.

When presenting your work, try to keep it concise. Highlight the challenges you overcame and the creative choices you made. The goal is to give them a glimpse into your thought process, problem-solving skills, workflows, contributions, and growth as an artist.

10.4.6 Dress Code

Figuring out what to wear for an interview can feel like a balancing act. The culture is often more laid-back than most, but you still want to show you're serious about the opportunity. No need for full formal wear, but showing up like you just rolled out of bed? Probably not the best move.

Go for something clean, professional, and casually smart. If you love video games (like most of us), a themed tee can actually be a good conversation starter. Just steer clear of anything offensive or overly edgy.

If you're unsure, check the studio's website, social channels, or team photos. It'll give you a sense of how people dress there.

And for remote interviews? The same rules apply. Keep it clean and professional, at least for what's visible on camera.

10.4.7 Communication

As mentioned before, how you communicate says a lot about you. In an interview, that's even more important. It's your chance to show not just what you know but how you think, work, and grow. It's not just what you say but *how* you say it. Keep your message clear and simple, and explain your process so anyone can understand.

Rather than listing your skills one by one, explain how you've actually used them. Saying "I know Unreal Engine" isn't enough – but walking someone through how you used it on a project? That lands. Put your skills in context, especially the ones that line up with what they're hiring for. That's how you stand out.

By the time you're in the interview, your portfolio and experience have already done most of the heavy lifting. That's what got you through the door. Now, the focus shifts to how you think, how you solve problems, and what it's like to work with you. Because in a collaborative setting, your soft skills matter just as much. Being great to work with is every bit as important as being great at what you do.

If you've got specialized skills or experience that is relevant – like a unique art style or experience with new tools – bring it up. When your abilities align with their needs, you're not just a candidate; you're a great fit.

Finally, steer clear of sensitive or divisive topics like politics. Keep the conversation professional and focused on your work and experience.

> *"A strong candidate is someone who shows motivation, remains open-minded, and is always ready to learn new things. Communication is key, but being a good listener is important too."*
>
> – Florian Guillaud

10.4.8 Adding Value

Employers want to see *you* – the real person behind the CV and portfolio. They're looking for someone who brings more than just know-how; they also want someone who fits well with the team.

So don't hold back on sharing what makes you, well, *you.* Your hobbies, your interests, even the little quirks you have – they all count.

Maybe you're into fantasy books, love board games, or have a thing for photography. Whatever it is, that stuff can help build a connection with your interviewer. And sometimes, those personal interests end up being exactly what the company needs, even if you didn't expect it.

10.4.9 Closing Strong

And finally, how you leave an interview is just as important as how you show up. This is where you leave your final impression, and it sticks more than you think.

As things wrap up, take a moment to thank your interviewers for their time, and let them know you're genuinely excited about the role.

And after that? Send a short follow-up thank-you message. Doesn't have to be fancy – just thoughtful, but more on that in a second.

10.5 WHAT'S NEXT?

So, the interview's done, and it's time to take a breather. Unless you've got more interviews lined up, in which case, it's time to prep again. Either way, you'll likely find yourself waiting for a response, and if you're like me, probably checking your inbox every five minutes. But what should you do next?

First things first: send a thank-you note. It doesn't need to be long – just a short, sincere message within 24 hours. Thank them for their time, mention something specific from the interview, and briefly express your continued interest. Two or three sentences are perfect. For example:

> "Thank you for the opportunity to interview for the [Job Title] position. I enjoyed our chat about [specific topic], and I'm even more excited about the possibility of joining the team."

Email is the standard, but if you're already connected on LinkedIn – or plan to connect – sending your thank-you as a direct message can feel more personal.

If they gave you a timeline for when you'll hear back, stick to that. If not, and a week or two passes with no word, it's fine to send a polite follow-up:

> "I wanted to follow up on my application for the [Job Title] position. I'm still very excited about the opportunity and would love any updates on the next steps."

If they say they're still deciding, respect it. Don't blow up their inbox, as that usually does more harm than good.

After all that, take some time to think back on how it went. What went well? What could you do better next time? That kind of self-reflection will only make you stronger for the next interview, no matter the outcome.

And hey, if you get the job? Awesome. Show your gratitude and excitement. If not, don't let it get you down. Still send a thank-you to appreciate the opportunity and their time. You always want to leave a good impression because you never know when another opportunity might come along.

Dealing with Rejection

11

Rejection sucks, especially when you're just starting out and working hard for that breakthrough. I remember back when I first started, sending out over a hundred applications for an internship myself and landing only two offers. It's rough.

What really matters is that you don't give up. Don't let rejection stop you. Instead, let's talk about how to deal with it, learn from it, and turn it into fuel to keep pushing forward.

11.1 DON'T TAKE IT PERSONALLY

Rejection can feel like a punch to the gut, especially after you've poured your heart and soul into your portfolio, art test, or interview. But here's the truth: it's not always a reflection of your talent or potential. More often, it comes down to timing, logistics, or internal factors you'll never see. Maybe the company already had someone in mind, or they needed someone with a very specific skill set. Sometimes, hiring someone from overseas means dealing with visas, relocation, legal hoops, and longer onboarding – which can make companies hesitant, even if you're a killer candidate. It doesn't mean you're not good enough – just that this wasn't the one.

Rejections happen all the time. Even the most experienced professionals face setbacks, missed opportunities, and yes, moments of self-doubt. What really matters, though, is not letting those rejections define you.

Being good enough is just the baseline. Success takes time, patience, knowing how to present yourself, and sometimes a bit of luck. So, instead of seeing rejections as a dead end, treat them as opportunities to improve, adapt, and keep moving forward.

DOI: 10.1201/9781003492320-11

11.2 STAY PROFESSIONAL

I know it's frustrating when you don't get the response you hoped for – or worse, when you don't hear anything at all. What you do in response says a lot about you. It's tempting to vent on social media or fire off a frustrated message to the studio, but honestly, that can backfire. The game industry is tight-knit, and one negative comment in public can burn bridges before you even know it.

So here's a better move – and yes, I mentioned this in the previous chapter too, because it's important: send a simple thank-you. Appreciate their time, and let them know you're open to future opportunities. That kind of professionalism, when things don't work out, says a lot about you. Hiring managers remember people who handle rejection with professionalism and respect.

It's okay to feel down – that's natural. But don't let it take over. Take the time you need, then get back up, refocus, and keep going. Every challenge moves you one step closer to where you want to be.

11.3 ASK FOR FEEDBACK

One of the smartest moves you can make after rejection? Ask for feedback. I know, it's not always the easiest thing to do when you're feeling down. But asking shows you're serious about improving – and that's a big deal.

Getting feedback gives you a clearer picture of what worked and what didn't. Sometimes, you'll hear things you never even considered, which can seriously boost your next try.

After you get the feedback, be sure to thank them again. Then, take some time to really think it through. What can you do differently? Polish your portfolio? Practice your answers? Learn a new skill? Whatever it is, use that feedback as your roadmap to grow and get closer to your goals.

One thing to know: sometimes companies won't give feedback. It's normal, especially with the flood of applications they get or legal stuff they have to consider. If you don't hear back, don't sweat it. Keep moving forward. The fact that you ask for feedback already sets you apart from the majority.

11.4 ANALYZE AND IMPROVE

Every time you hit a wall, there's a chance to learn and come back stronger – but only if you take the time to reflect.

If you didn't get to the interview stage, start by revisiting your application and assessing where things might have gone wrong. Was your portfolio actually tailored toward the role? Did it show off your strongest, most relevant work that lines up with what they need? And be honest: were you maybe reaching too far too soon? Sometimes, it's about finding the right fit before shooting for the stars.

Then, check your CV. Did it clearly lay out your skills and experience in a way that grabbed attention? Was it easy to see why you'd be a good match? And what about your cover letter – did it show you understood what the studio's all about and what they're looking for? Did it show you're excited about the role and how your goals connect to theirs?

Now, if you made it to the interview stage but still got passed over, that can sting – especially if you had to do an art test or put in extra time. But hey, making it that far means you've got something going on. Don't stop there. Think back on how you came across. Did you answer their questions clearly and with confidence? Or did some of them trip you up? Were there technical bits you stumbled on? It's not just about the answers, but it's also about how you present yourself – your enthusiasm, your adaptability, and why you're the person they want on their team.

Break it all down. What worked? What didn't? The more you reflect, the sharper you get – and the more ready you'll be when the next opportunity shows up.

11.5 KEEP APPLYING

Just like anything else, the more you practice, the better you get. Every single application is a chance to refine your strategy, polish your CV, sharpen your skills, and build a stronger portfolio. The most important thing? Keep applying.

Don't limit yourself to one company or role. Apply to different companies, different roles, and maybe even other CG-related fields like film, architecture, or medical visualization. You might be more qualified than you think. Just make sure your portfolio fits the job and you're passionate about the role. The more flexible you are, the more doors will open.

If you're really set on a particular company you've applied to before, reapply once you've improved your skills. Nobody can improve themselves overnight. The general recommendation is to wait at least three to six months before reapplying. This gives you enough time to improve your skills, build a stronger portfolio, and ensure that your application is more aligned with the company's needs. But if you've made significant progress faster, go ahead and try again sooner.

And remember, don't spam a company or person if you don't hear back. Sending multiple applications or follow-ups won't get you anywhere. Use that time to level up your skills, polish your application, and come back stronger.

Every application moves you forward. Keep pushing, learn from each experience, and trust that persistence will pay off. Keep applying because the right opportunity is out there waiting for you.

11.6 STAYING THE COURSE

Finding a job takes time. With layoffs and industry shifts, many established professionals spend months – sometimes years – searching before landing their next role. If you really want to work in games, you have to be resilient.

Along the way, it's important to celebrate the small wins. Maybe you landed an interview at a studio you've admired forever. Or maybe you got solid feedback that pushed your portfolio up a notch. These are milestones worth acknowledging. They may not immediately result in a job offer, but they are clear signs that you're making progress. Celebrating these moments will help you stay motivated and boost your confidence.

At the end of the day, remember that every rejection is just one step closer to where you want to be. It's easy to feel discouraged in the moment, but with time, persistence, self-reflection, and a refined approach, you'll get there. Your dream job isn't a matter of "if" but "when." Keep pushing, stay open to learning, and trust that all the effort you're putting in will eventually pay off. If others can do it, so can you. You've got this.

Contracts and Salary

12

Landing a job is exciting, but it's just as important to understand the terms of your employment. Why? Because a solid contract and fair salary are the foundation of a sustainable career. They ensure that you're respected, valued, and treated fairly as a professional. So, while the business side of things might seem a bit dull, don't underestimate how much of an impact it can have.

12.1 SALARY EXPECTATIONS

Let's talk numbers first because this part can feel tricky if you don't know where to start.

Salaries in games vary wildly. Location, experience, and studio all play a role. A game artist at a big AAA studio in the United States might earn far more than someone at a small indie team in Eastern Europe, where living costs are generally lower.

Here's where it gets complicated: many studios still keep their salary details private, making it hard to know if you're getting paid fairly. Some even prohibit employees from discussing pay. That's changing, though. Some countries and states now have laws that require companies to post salary ranges in their job listings. Sounds good, right? But even those ranges can still be very broad.

While sites like Glassdoor and LinkedIn can offer a broad sense of anonymously shared salary information, I wanted a more focused, industry-specific perspective for this book. That's why I reached out to Skillsearch, a recruitment agency specializing in games and interactive industries. Every year, they run the *Games & Interactive Salary & Satisfaction Survey*, where developers can anonymously share their insights. They kindly let me use the results from their most recent survey (as of writing) – covering 2024/2025 and published in 2025 – to supplement this book. You can find reproduced charts of their findings in Figures 12.1–12.4. The charts shown represent global data, which has been converted to Great Britain Pound (GBP) for consistency.

DOI: 10.1201/9781003492320-12

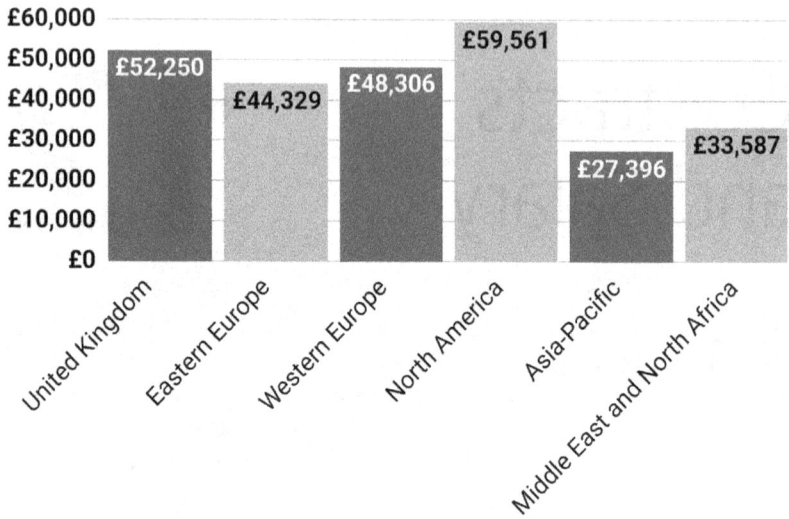

FIGURE 12.1 Average annual salaries by continent.

Source: Based on data from Skillsearch's 2024/25 Salary & Satisfaction Survey, used with permission. Salaries are shown in GBP for consistency.

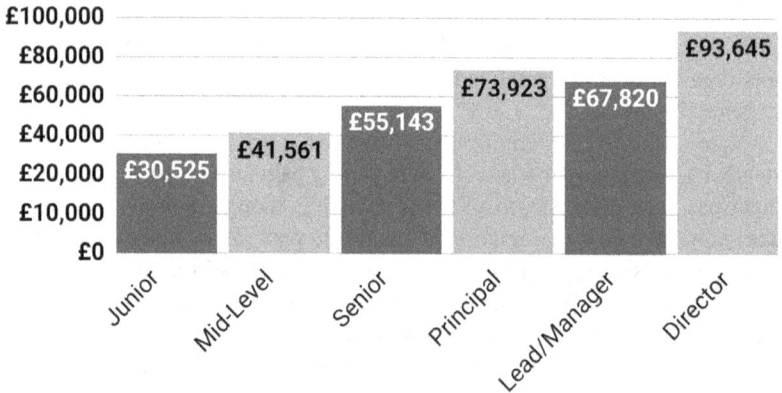

FIGURE 12.2 Average annual salaries by seniority level.

Source: Based on data from Skillsearch's 2024/25 Salary & Satisfaction Survey, used with permission. Salaries are shown in GBP for consistency.

	£59,817	£55,132	£59,346

£60,000
£40,000
£20,000
£0

Console   Mobile   PC

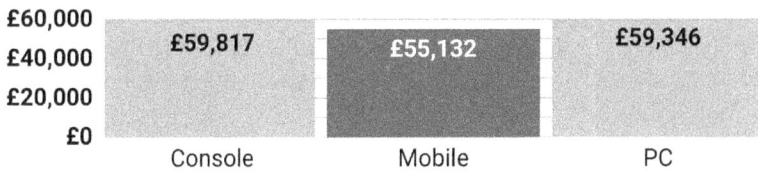

FIGURE 12.3   Average annual salaries by platform.

Source: Based on data from Skillsearch's 2024/25 Salary & Satisfaction Survey, used with permission. Salaries are shown in GBP for consistency.

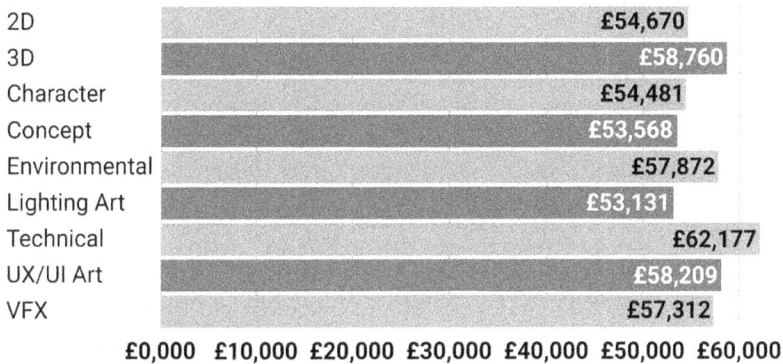

	Salary
2D	£54,670
3D	£58,760
Character	£54,481
Concept	£53,568
Environmental	£57,872
Lighting Art	£53,131
Technical	£62,177
UX/UI Art	£58,209
VFX	£57,312

£0,000 £10,000 £20,000 £30,000 £40,000 £50,000 £60,000

FIGURE 12.4   Average annual salaries by art specialization.

Source: Based on data from Skillsearch's 2024/25 Salary & Satisfaction Survey, used with permission. Salaries are shown in GBP for consistency.

Keep in mind, these data reflect conditions from 2024/2025. Salaries shift over time due to inflation, market demand, and economic changes. Use the charts as a rough guide, not a rulebook. What matters most is understanding your value, evaluating offers realistically, and learning how to negotiate with confidence.

Also, remember, salary is just one part of the picture. Benefits like health care, vacation time, retirement contributions, flexible hours, and remote work all play a role, too. Some companies also offer bonuses, wellness programs, or even stock options.

So next time you're reviewing a job offer, don't just zero in on the base salary. Think about the whole package – benefits, perks, and everything that adds up. Once you know what's fair and what you're worth, negotiate for it.

12.2 NEGOTIATION

Negotiating your employment terms is a critical skill in any field – game art included. But before you even think about talking numbers, you need to know your value – not just in terms of salary but in terms of the value you can bring to a company.

So, what do you bring to the table? Be honest with yourself. What are your strengths? Maybe you're a character artist with a talent for real-time hair or a concept artist who knows exactly how your designs will seamlessly translate into 3D.

Then, there's your experience. Have you worked on games before? Freelanced? Created standout personal projects, or collaborated on team ones? That stuff matters and sometimes weighs more than how well you can use the latest tools.

Don't just think about the technical stuff either. Your soft skills – like collaboration, problem-solving, and consistently hitting deadlines – are just as valuable.

When the offer comes, don't be afraid to advocate for yourself. I know money talks can feel intimidating, but if they've decided they want you, asking for what you're worth won't scare them off. Worst case? They say there's no wiggle room. But in the best-case scenario? You might walk away with a higher salary, a signing bonus, extra perks, or maybe even a better role than you thought possible.

Before you walk into any negotiation, you need to have your numbers locked in, not just what sounds nice, but what actually works for you. There are three numbers you'll want to figure out ahead of time:

- **Your minimum number**: This is your baseline – the number you *can't* go below without putting yourself in a tough spot. If the offer lands under this, it's a no. No hard feelings. Just not sustainable.
- **Your comfortable number**: This is your middle ground – enough to live well, cover your expenses, save a bit, and not stress every time rent or a bill comes due.
- **Your ideal number**: This is your stretch goal – the number that reflects your full value: your skills, experience, what you bring to the table, and maybe a little extra to grow your savings. You might not always get it, but it's worth aiming for.

Recruiters will ask about your salary expectations, so make sure you have a clear range in mind. Lead with your ideal number. That's your starting point, the number that reflects what you believe your time, skills, and experience are worth. If they push back? No problem. You can slide toward your comfortable range. But don't drop too quickly, and don't sell yourself short. This is a conversation, not a test. And whatever you do, don't go below your minimum. That number is for you *only*. Keep it in your back pocket, but never put it on the table. That's your line, and it's nonnegotiable.

Also, keep in mind that the salary you negotiate isn't what ends up in your bank account. Taxes, health care, and pension contributions will chip away at it, and these vary depending on where you live. So before you get too excited, do the math. Look up local deductions. If you're moving cities or countries, check the cost of living. What sounds great in one place might fall short elsewhere. And be sure to factor in other expenses too – commuting, housing, and visa fees (some companies cover these, but it's worth asking). You can use tools like Payscale or Numbeo to help you gauge if the offer matches local costs and supports the lifestyle you want.

You don't have to accept the offer on the spot, either. It's completely okay to ask for a bit of time to think it over. Let them know you appreciate the offer and that you'll get back to them as soon as possible – ideally by the end of the day or the following day at the latest. It's a big decision, and it's important to be sure.

If you have other interviews lined up in the next few days, you might want to wait and see how those play out – but be aware that waiting too long could mean losing the current offer entirely. Some studios move quickly, and they may not hold a spot open for long.

Sometimes, mentioning that you have other interviews lined up can give you additional leverage. If they know other studios are interested, they may be more willing to bump up the offer rather than risk losing you to someone else. Just be honest and respectful – the goal isn't to pressure them but to give them a clear picture of your situation.

At the end of the day, your salary should match the skills, experience, and value you bring to the company. The market can be competitive, but that doesn't mean you should settle for less. Do your homework. Know your worth. And don't be afraid to ask for it.

12.3 TYPES OF CONTRACTS

Once you've agreed on a salary, the next thing heading your way is the contract. In most cases, you'll be offered either a fixed-term or a full-time (permanent) contract. Both are common in the industry, and each comes with its own advantages. Let's take a closer look at what they mean so you can figure out which suits you best.

12.3.1 Fixed-Term

A fixed-term contract means you're hired for a set period, with clearly defined start and end dates. This type of contract is very common in the industry, especially if you're just starting out or being brought in temporarily to support a particular project – like creating assets or helping out during a busy production phase.

What's great about fixed-term contracts is that you know exactly how long you're signed up for. That makes planning your next steps a bit easier. It's also a solid way to jump between studios or projects, build your portfolio, and grow your skills without long-term commitment.

But here's the catch: once the contract ends, there's no guarantee of what's next. You might have a gap between jobs unless you've already got another opportunity lined up. Sometimes, studios offer the option to go permanent, but don't count on it. Also, benefits tend to be better with full-time roles, so be sure to review the offer carefully before signing anything.

12.3.2 Full-Time

Unlike fixed-term contracts, a full-time permanent contract doesn't have a set end date. It usually comes with more stability: steady income, ongoing employment, and access to benefits like health insurance, paid leave, and retirement plans.

It's also a great way to build a career at one studio. You'll get to work on different projects, grow your skills, and maybe climb the ladder into senior or leadership roles. (Though switching studios can also be a solid strategy to advance your career.)

That said, full-time jobs often come with some strings attached. Many studios expect you to work exclusively for them, so side gigs might not be allowed – or you'll need written permission, like I had to get for writing this book. So, if you like having the freedom to work on multiple things at once, that's something to keep in mind.

12.4 GETTING READY TO START

Getting the job doesn't end with signing the contract. Now it's time to get everything lined up so you can hit the ground running. Whether you're moving across the country or just switching cities, getting job-ready means more than showing up on day one.

If you're moving to a new country, handle the paperwork early. Visas, work permits, and residency documents can take weeks or months to process. Some companies will walk you through it; others leave it to you. Either way, don't wait – starting early makes your transition smoother. Also, don't forget to update things like health care, bank accounts, and utilities early to avoid last-minute headaches.

Some companies offer relocation packages for flights, moving costs, or short-term housing. If it's not mentioned, don't hesitate to ask. The worst they can say is no, but the best-case scenario is you save money. If no support's available, budget carefully. Deposits, movers, furniture, and visa fees all can add up quickly. Planning ahead helps avoid surprises.

You also want to double-check your start date and make sure everyone's on the same page. Some want you on-site immediately, while others are more flexible. If you need extra time to relocate or wrap things up, ask for it. Most employers understand that relocating isn't something you do overnight. In fact, arriving a few days or even a couple of weeks early can give you a buffer to settle in, explore, adjust to a new time zone, and catch your breath before the job officially begins.

Working as a Game Artist: Day-to-Day

13

So, what's it actually like to work as a game artist? In this chapter, we'll walk through what a typical day might look like, what meetings to expect, how you collaborate with other departments, and why something as simple as file naming matters more than you'd think. You'll also get familiar with the software and tools artists use in game development (yes, there are a few), how tasks are tracked, and what it's like to work within the pressure of deadlines and sprints.

13.1 STUDIO ENVIRONMENT

If you're not working from home, you'll likely be in the studio's office. While every company has its own culture, many studios share similar features. Studio size can play a big role; larger ones often offer more facilities and perks in comparison to smaller ones.

Workspaces vary widely from one company to another, too. Some use cubicles; others prefer open floor plans to encourage teamwork. Desks are often decorated with personal memorabilia, action figures, posters, and other collectibles that reflect the personalities of the team. Don't be surprised if someone's desk looks more like a shrine to their favorite franchise than a typical workspace.

Some studios even allow pets. It's not unusual to see a dog napping under a desk or trotting through the hallways. Dogs tend to be the most common office companions – I haven't met a studio cat yet, but never say never.

Then, there's the kitchen. It's typically stocked with coffee, tea, fruit, and snacks to fuel your day. Some studios go further, offering catered meals or a

DOI: 10.1201/9781003492320-13

full cafeteria. These spaces become natural gathering points for casual chats, coffee breaks, or lunch with colleagues.

With a shared interest in games and media, many studios keep libraries of books, games, and movies for employees to borrow. Some have game rooms with consoles, ping-pong or pool tables, and retro arcade machines. Studios also often host board game nights as a way for employees to relax and socialize after hours.

Others go the extra mile with on-site gyms or fitness classes like yoga and stretching. At one studio, I even joined weekly MMA training sessions with a few colleagues. Light, friendly sparring (with gloves, of course) was a fun way to blow off steam after long hours at the desk.

Dress codes are generally casual. Most people wear jeans, shorts, hoodies, or t-shirts – including management. Formal wear is rare and typically reserved for special events or client meetings, if at all. Some people swap shoes for slippers, and yes, pajama pants do make the occasional appearance – but maybe hold off on that for day one. While most studios keep things laid-back, expectations vary. Professionalism still matters, especially when clients are involved or in more formal environments.

Finally, security is a priority. Most studios require chip badges or key cards for entry. Access is restricted to protect sensitive projects, and certain areas may only be accessible to specific team members.

13.2 TYPICAL WORKDAY

A typical workday can look a bit different depending on where you work and the specific role you're in, but some patterns show up across the board.

In most game studios, working hours are flexible. Rather than a strict 9-to-5, many teams have core hours in place when everyone is expected to be available – say, between 10:00 AM and 2:00 PM, but that also can vary per studio. Outside of those hours, you're often free to manage your time and schedule as you see fit.

After your first cup of coffee or tea, it's time to check your emails and messages. Depending on your team, there might be a stand-up meeting to sync up with your colleagues, share progress, and discuss any issues.

Once the day gets rolling, you'll focus on your main tasks – drawing concepts, creating 3D models, refining textures, or building environments, depending on your role. While focusing on your work, you'll often collaborate closely with teammates and other departments, making adjustments based on feedback.

Throughout the day, it's common to take short breaks – to stretch your legs, grab another coffee, or chat with a teammate – especially during long periods of focused work.

Alongside your creative tasks, meetings are a regular part of the week. These often cluster on Mondays, when teams align on goals, plan tasks, and set priorities for the week. Some studios spread meetings more evenly to keep Mondays light. The frequency depends on the studio, the team, your role, and the project: some weeks are packed with meetings, while others are more focused and quiet.

By the end of the day, you might have a final round of meetings to review progress, adjust priorities, and take care of anything urgent before a looming deadline. If all goes well, you'll wrap things up by checking off what you've done, setting your plan for tomorrow, and calling it a day.

13.3 MEETINGS

If you're working for a game studio, meetings will be a regular part of your routine. They might not be everyone's favorite, but they're not as bad as you think. In fact, they're the glue that holds everything together.

Think of them as checkpoints, not just calendar clutter. When done right, meetings help keep the team aligned, the project moving forward, and communication clear. It's how we stay connected in the chaos we call game development.

That said, not all meetings are the same. Some are quick check-ins; others dive deep into design decisions, and then, there are the ones where you walk out feeling like your brain just melted.

Here's a quick rundown of common meetings you'll likely face during development:

13.3.1 Core Development

- **Daily Stand-ups** – Short morning check-ins to share what you're working on, any blockers, and overall progress. These keep the team aligned and help spot issues early.
- **Weekly Syncs** – Longer catchups to review progress, plan the week ahead, and flag any challenges. These are great for resetting priorities and checking in on broader goals.

- **Art Dailies/Reviews** – Daily or semi-regular meetings where artists present work to the team or art leads. These help ensure consistency in art direction and give space for constructive feedback.
- **Feedback Sessions** – Review work with leads or directors to get constructive input and align closely with the creative vision. These can be one-on-one or group-focused.
- **Cross-Disciplinary Syncs** – Team-wide meetings that bring together art, design, programming, and other departments to align efforts, ensure smooth integration, and maintain clear communication across disciplines.

13.3.2 Problem-Solving and Iteration

- **Problem-Solving Meetings** – Focused discussions to troubleshoot urgent technical or design issues. These usually pop up as needed and often include tech artists or engineers.
- **Internal Playtests** – Team-wide gameplay sessions to test how everything – gameplay, visuals, and narrative – comes together. These help artists see their work in context and catch issues early.

13.3.3 Studio Milestones and Syncs

- **Retrospectives** – Regular reflection meetings held after sprints or smaller phases. These focus on what went well, what didn't, and how to improve.
- **Post-mortems** – Broader reviews held after major milestones or project completion to evaluate outcomes and apply lessons learned moving forward.
- **Show and Tell/Demo Days** – Informal team presentations to share cool new work, celebrate wins, and stay inspired. These can range from small internal demos to bigger studio-wide showcases.
- **Studio-Wide Briefings** – Studio-wide updates from leadership about company direction, goals, upcoming projects, and studio culture. These help everyone feel connected to the bigger picture.

13.3.4 Personal Growth and Development

- **One-on-Ones** – Personal check-ins with your lead to talk about career growth, current challenges, and how you're doing overall. A space to get support and discuss your development path.

- **Evaluations** – Periodic reviews (usually done quarterly or biannually) to go over performance, goals, and future opportunities. These are often tied to raises, promotions, or personal growth plans.

13.3.5 External Collaboration

- **Client/Stakeholder Meetings** – Present work and get feedback from external partners or publishers. These are more common in outsourcing, live service games, or publisher-facing roles.

13.4 TASK MANAGEMENT

Task management is important for development teams to stay organized and meet deadlines. Most studios use tools like Jira or Trello (which we'll cover later in this chapter) to track progress, assign work, and set priorities. These tools break down big tasks into smaller, manageable pieces, making it easier to track and avoid feeling overwhelmed. Each task is typically given a priority level – such as *lowest*, *low*, *medium*, *high,* or *highest* – to help teams focus on what matters most.

Tasks usually begin in a backlog, a pool of upcoming work. For each sprint or phase, selected tasks are moved into "to-do." Your lead typically assigns tasks to you based on the team's needs and your individual strengths. When you start working on a task, it's moved to "in progress." Once completed, it shifts to "to test" or "review" for feedback. If everything checks out, it's marked "completed." If revisions are needed, it's reassigned and returned to the responsible person. This system helps teams track progress clearly and catch blockers early.

Since game studios often work under tight deadlines, tackling high-priority tasks first is important. It's usually the project manager, producer, or team lead who decides what's urgent and what can wait.

13.5 WORKING UNDER DEADLINES

Deadlines – love them or hate them, but they're inevitable. If you've been in school, you know the drill. Learning to work within deadlines is an essential skill every artist should have.

When estimating how long a task will take, always plan some extra time for the unexpected. For example, if you think a model will take you about a week to complete, plan for an extra day or two just in case. Mistakes, revisions, and tech issues happen all the time. If you don't account for that buffer, you'll end up stressed, rushed, and scrambling to deliver.

If you realize partway through a task that you might need more time, communicate this to your lead as soon as possible. For instance, you could say, *"Hey, I'm running into some challenges with this asset. I estimate I'll need an extra day to polish it – can we adjust the schedule?"* Clear communication like this helps avoid surprises and builds trust within your team.

Not every asset will be perfect by the deadline. That's normal. Instead, focus on what matters: which assets need detail and which can be simplified without compromising quality. For example, a main character model that is front and center typically requires more polish than a background prop that's viewed only from a distance. Managing scope is how you meet deadlines without losing too much.

That's also where efficiency comes into play. Speed isn't just about working faster but smarter. Learn shortcuts in Photoshop, Maya, Substance Painter, or whatever you use. Don't hesitate to pick up new tips from colleagues or online tutorials; there's always a quicker way to do something. Automate repetitive tasks where you can. The more friction you remove from your process, the more time and energy you'll have for the creative work that matters.

Messy files and disorganized folders can also slow you down. Keep everything clean and clearly labeled. Revisions are inevitable, and digging through clutter wastes time. Also, keeping folders and projects organized makes collaboration smoother when teammates need to jump into your files. It's a small effort with a big payoff.

Even with a strong workflow, one of the most common pitfalls when working under pressure is falling into isolation. It's easy to go heads-down and hope you're on track. Don't. Check in regularly with leads, the team, or clients. Early feedback avoids last-minute surprises.

13.6 WORKING WITH OTHER DEPARTMENTS

In game development, teams rarely work in isolation, and that includes artists. While your daily work focuses on creating art, you're always contributing to a larger whole.

Every asset – character, environment, or animation – connects to someone else's work. Maybe it supports a game mechanic, integrates into a narrative moment, or needs to run efficiently within a complex system. Understanding this broader context helps your art align with the game's vision, both creatively and technically.

Working with other departments means being open to feedback beyond just art. You may need to adjust a design to support performance, gameplay clarity, or production timelines. These changes aren't personal; they're part of building a coherent, functioning product. It's important to stay flexible and willing to iterate when new information comes in.

Different disciplines often have their own terminology, priorities, and workflows. Learning how to speak each other's language – or at least asking clarifying questions – can prevent misunderstandings and reduce frustration on both sides. Being approachable, responsive, and proactive builds trust and makes collaboration with other departments smoother.

If you're unsure how your work fits the bigger picture, talk to your lead. It's also important to keep them in the loop when receiving feedback from others, as acting on someone else's feedback without coordination can disrupt planning.

13.7 FILE NAMING AND ORGANIZATION

We've all done it – saved a file as texture1.jpg on an already cluttered desktop, or worse, named it something like finalFINAL_reallyFinal_v7.obj (which, to be honest, sounds like it could double as a password) and then buried it in a folder you'll never find again.

In game development, where projects stretch for years and involve thousands of assets, good organization is crucial. It keeps workflows smooth and makes iterating, troubleshooting, and collaborating easier. The more complex the project, the more critical it becomes.

You're not just managing your own workflow; you're making sure others can quickly understand and use your files too. Ideally, someone should be able to open your files and instantly know what they're looking at – no guesswork or endless clicking through folders.

Most studios have naming conventions and folder structures in place. Always ask about them up front and follow them closely. These aren't arbitrary rules; they avoid confusion and help the team collaborate smoothly. Keeping a printed reference sheet of these conventions at your desk during your first few weeks can help you avoid mistakes and build good habits.

Good organization on your local machine is important, but when you're collaborating across departments or on shared projects, things need to be even more robust. That's where version control comes in.

13.7.1 Version Control

If you've ever lost a file, overwritten someone else's work, or spent too long digging through disorganized folders, you already know why version control matters. Fun fact: back in high school, when sharing files with friends, we'd bury files so deep in useless folders (like a dungeon crawler) just for laughs. Fun then, but definitely not something you want to do professionally.

Version control (or source control) acts as both a safety net and a traffic controller. It keeps projects stable and organized, especially when multiple people work in parallel. While the terms are often used interchangeably, *version control* refers more broadly to systems that track changes to files over time, whereas *source control* traditionally refers to managing changes to source code – though in game development, they usually mean the same thing. Whether a solo project or a studio production, version control lets everyone build together without stepping on each other's toes.

Tools like Git, Perforce, or SVN track every change to every file, saving them systematically. You can see who changed what, when, and why. If something breaks (and it will), you can roll back to a working version. That alone can be a lifesaver when you're experimenting or working under tight deadlines.

Branching is one of version control's most powerful features. It lets someone work on their own copy (fixing a bug, modifying an asset, or adding a feature) without affecting the main build. Once tested, their work merges back safe and clean.

This is especially helpful when multiple people edit the same files. Imagine two artists unknowingly tweaking the same texture – version control flags those conflicts and helps resolve them before things get messy.

Think of version control as a time machine. Made a mistake weeks ago, or something stopped working? You can compare versions to track down the cause. It gives you the freedom to iterate and take risks, knowing you can always go back to a working state.

Version control might seem intimidating at first, especially if you're used to working solo. But once you get the hang of it, it quickly becomes second nature.

13.8 EQUIPMENT

Game development tools aren't exactly light. They eat up memory, demand high processing power, and don't always play nice with old or underpowered machines. If you've ever dealt with a laggy viewport or a crash mid-save, you know the frustration. A solid computer won't fix everything, but it'll save you tons of headaches.

If you work in a studio, most of the heavy lifting is handled for you. IT usually provides a powerful, preconfigured PC, one or two monitors, and peripherals like a graphics tablet, keyboard, and mouse. These machines are typically built to handle heavy software like 3D modeling programs, digital painting tools, and game engines without breaking (much of) a sweat.

If you work remotely full-time, studios often ship gear or offer a budget to set up your workspace. Hybrid roles (a mix of in-office and remote work) usually get a high-end gaming laptop for portability without losing too much power. This mostly applies to salaried employees, not freelancers. As a freelancer, you're an independent contractor – meaning your tools, equipment, licenses, and workspace are all on you.

13.9 SOFTWARE AND TOOLS

Let's look at some industry-standard tools commonly used in the industry and frequently listed in job postings. Will you use all of them? Probably not. The tools you work with depend on your role, focus, and studio. But knowing what's out there can give you a solid head start.

Many of these tools do similar things in slightly different ways. If you understand the core principles – say, of modeling or sculpting – you'll find those same foundations carry over from one tool to another. Often, it's just the UI that changes. One feature might be front and center in one app and buried under a drop-down menu in another. Once you're familiar with how the tools work, switching between them gets way less intimidating.

So don't stress about learning everything now. Focus on building your skills and experimenting. The tools will follow.

13.9.1 Communication

Games are made by teams, and teams run on communication. You might be an environment artist sharing progress with level designers or a character artist coordinating with riggers – communication is part of the job, whether you're sitting across the room or working from another time zone.

- **Slack** – Slack is a team communication platform developed by Slack Technologies, now part of Salesfore. It's like your digital office watercooler – with channels. It's built for teams to chat, share files, and stay organized without drowning in emails. You can have topic-specific channels, send DMs, drop GIFs, or even jump on quick calls. A lot of game studios rely on Slack because it's clean, fast, and integrates well with tools like Jira, Google Drive, and more.
- **Mattermost** – Mattermost is an open-source team messaging plat-form developed by Mattermost Inc. It looks and works similarly to Slack, but it's self-hosted, meaning companies can control their data more tightly. If you've used Slack, you'll feel right at home here.
- **Discord** – Discord is a communication platform developed by Discord Inc. It started out as a go-to app for gamers, and it still holds that reputation. Discord has also found a solid place in profes-sional settings, especially in indie studios and creative communities. Channels are easy to set up, video calls are quick, and screen shar-ing is seamless. While it's not as "corporate" as Slack or Teams, a lot of indie teams, student groups, or smaller studios use it to stay connected.
- **Microsoft Teams** – Microsoft Teams is a collaboration and messag-ing platform developed by Microsoft. If your studio uses Microsoft 365, you'll probably end up using Teams. It brings together mes-saging, video calls, file sharing, and calendar integration all in one place. What makes Teams stand out is how tightly it connects with tools like Outlook, Word, Excel, and SharePoint, making collabora-tion super streamlined if you're already in that ecosystem.
- **Zoom** – Zoom is a video conferencing tool developed by Zoom Video Communications. It became a trusted tool during the remote work boom, and it's still going strong. It's especially useful for team meetings, interviews, or guest speaker sessions. You'll find features like breakout rooms (smaller group sessions within a larger call), recording, screen sharing, and virtual backgrounds. While it's not built for everyday messaging, its strength lies in the high video and audio quality, reliable screen sharing, and the ability to host large group calls without much hassle.

- **Google Meet** – Google Meet is a video communication tool developed by Google as part of Google Workspace. It's tied into Gmail and Google Calendar, so if your studio uses Google Workspace, chances are your meetings will happen here. It's simple, quick to launch, and works well in-browser.

13.9.2 Tracking and Management

There are many tracking and management tools out there, and studios tend to choose what works best for their workflow. Broadly speaking, these ensure that teams are aligned, tasks are completed on time, and assets are properly versioned (saved in clear versions so it's always clear which is the latest). They help artists, designers, programmers, and everyone else collaborate smoothly and stay up to date on the project's progress.

- **Perforce** – Perforce is the industry shorthand for the Helix Core version control system and its graphical interface, Helix Visual Client (also known as P4 or P4V) – all developed by Perforce Software. While "Perforce" technically refers to the broader suite, it's commonly used to describe the whole system, especially the visual client that most artists and developers interact with.

    Perforce is a standard in the games industry, especially when you're dealing with large projects, big teams, and loads of assets. It's built to handle everything from code to large binary[1] files like textures, models, and animations. What makes Perforce stand out is how it lets artists, designers, and programmers all work simultaneously without overwriting each other's work, thanks to file locking and branching tools. That said, some smaller teams or code-focused projects might go with Git or SVN instead.
- **Jira** – Jira is a project management and issue tracking tool developed by Atlassian. It's widely used in the games industry to manage sprints, assign tasks, track bugs, and keep production on schedule. Jira is especially valued by producers and developers for its ability to organize complex workflows, support Agile methodologies, and maintain visibility across teams.
- **Confluence** – Confluence is another tool developed by Atlassian, focused on collaboration and documentation. It serves as a central hub for storing production notes, design documents, meeting summaries, and internal wikis. Confluence is often used alongside Jira, helping teams share knowledge, define pipelines, and stay aligned across departments. Its integration with Jira allows for seamless

linking between tasks and documentation, making it a core part of many game studios' production workflows.

- **ShotGrid** – ShotGrid (formerly Shotgun) is developed by Autodesk. It's a favorite tool in studios with heavy asset production and creative pipelines, especially in film, animation, and game development. Designed specifically for artists and production teams, it helps track every step of production – from initial concepts all the way to final renders. This makes it particularly useful for teams working in visual pipelines, helping manage assets, versions, and feedback efficiently.

  One super useful feature of ShotGrid is that it allows for annotations directly on images and even videos, so teams can leave precise feedback without having to rely on external tools.

- **Hansoft** – Hansoft is developed by Perforce Software (the same company behind Perforce version control). It has a solid presence in studios needing a hybrid approach for complex, cross-team planning. It sits between Jira and ShotGrid, blending Agile and Waterfall methods into one platform. Built to support both software teams and broader project coordination, Hansoft is often picked for high-level planning alongside real-time task tracking.

- **Trello** – Trello is a visual task management tool developed by Atlassian. It works like a digital bulletin board, where you can organize tasks into columns using cards that you can drag and drop. Its simplicity and flexibility make it ideal for quick task tracking, small team workflows, or managing personal to-do lists and side projects.

- **Notion** – Notion is a flexible workspace app developed by Notion Labs Inc. It combines note-taking, task management, databases, and wikis into one interface, making it an all-in-one solution for documentation and team collaboration. It's especially useful for keeping everything – from meeting notes and design guidelines to project timelines – in one place. Game development teams often use Notion to centralize production info without needing multiple disconnected tools.

- **Miro** – Miro is an online collaborative whiteboard developed by Miro (formerly RealtimeBoard). It's designed for brainstorming, mind-mapping, and real-time collaboration, especially in remote or hybrid work environments. With sticky notes, diagrams, and templates, it helps teams visually map out ideas, pipelines, or feature roadmaps. Miro is frequently used during planning phases, sprint kickoffs, and brainstorm sessions.

13.9.3 Game Engines

Like an engine that drives a car's motion, a game engine is the backbone of every video game. It runs all of the game's functionality, from the rendering of the characters and environments to the physics, animation, gameplay, and networking systems. Game engines provide developers with the tools they need to build a game.

Engines like *Unity* and *Unreal* are widely used across the industry for their versatility, ease of use, and extensive documentation. Some studios create their own proprietary game engine that is tailored to their specific needs, such as Guerrilla's *Decima* or Ubisoft's *Snowdrop* engine.

Choosing the right engine is important for a studio, as each has its own strengths and weaknesses that depend on the project, target platform, and the amount of experience the team has with the engine.

- **Unreal Engine** – Unreal Engine, developed by Epic Games, is known for its high-quality graphics, performance, and user-friendly tools. Fun fact: its name comes from *Unreal*, a first-person shooter from way back in 1998, which was the very first game to run on it.

  What makes Unreal Engine stand out is that it's like a full toolbox all in one place. You get 3D rendering, physics, animation, and more. One standout feature is Blueprint, a visual scripting system that lets artists and designers implement game logic without needing to code.

  With the release of Unreal Engine 5, things jumped to the next level thanks to breakthrough technologies like Nanite and Lumen. Nanite lets you render insanely detailed models, while Lumen handles lighting and reflections in real time, making everything look incredibly lifelike.

  Unreal also integrates with the FAB marketplace, a unified asset store that brings together content from Sketchfab, Quixel, ArtStation, and others, making it easier than ever to find and use high-quality assets directly within your project.

  And here's the kicker: Unreal isn't just for games anymore. It's increasingly used in TV, film, virtual production, architecture, and simulation. So the skills you pick up here can take you places far beyond game development.

- **Unity** – Unity, developed by Unity Technologies, has been around since 2005, and it's come a long way from its early days as a Mac-focused engine. Today, it's everywhere – from mobile games and indie projects to VR experiences and console hits.

Under the hood, Unity runs on C#, which gives you plenty of flexibility to build whatever gameplay systems you dream up. Some coding or scripting is required in Unity if you want to build anything advanced, but you don't need to be a coding expert to start. Unity's scripting is beginner-friendly, and there are tons of tutorials and resources to guide you through the basics. You can often get well on your way just by learning a few core concepts like variables, functions, and events.

That said, if you absolutely want to avoid coding, Unity offers built-in Visual Scripting (used to be called Bolt), which lets you build logic using a drag-and-drop system. It's great for prototyping, experimenting, or just thinking through problems visually.

Like Unreal Engine's FAB marketplace, Unity has its own resource hub – the Unity Asset Store. It's a massive library of ready-made tools, scripts, shaders, and art assets that can speed up development and lighten your workload.

13.9.4 Digital Content Creation

Game artists use a wide range of software, and what they choose usually comes down to their personal preferences, the kind of work they do, and what part of the process they're focused on – whether it's 2D art, 3D modeling, animation, texturing, or something else.

- **3ds Max** – Autodesk's 3ds Max is a full-featured 3D software package widely used in the film and game industry. First released in 1990, it's known for its robust modeling and animation tools, making it a popular choice for game development as well as architectural visualization. Artists can model, rig, texture, animate, and render complete scenes within the software.
- **Maya** – Also from Autodesk, Maya was released in 1998 and has become a leading tool in both game and film production. It's favored for character rigging, simulations, and high-end animation workflows. Like 3ds Max, Maya supports the full 3D pipeline, from modeling and rigging to animation and rendering.
- **Blender** – Blender, developed by the Blender Foundation, is a free, open-source 3D creation suite that's become increasingly popular in game development lately. It offers a full range of tools for modeling, sculpting, texturing, rigging, animation, and even video editing. While tools like Autodesk Maya and 3ds Max remain dominant

in many studios, Blender's no-cost license and active development community have made it a strong contender, especially among indie developers and smaller teams.

* **ZBrush** – ZBrush is a digital sculpting program developed by Pixologic and released in 2002. It allows artists to sculpt digitally as if working with real clay, offering a highly intuitive experience. With ZBrush, you can carve intricate surface details like wrinkles, pores, and fabric textures with incredible precision. It's widely used in both games and film for creating detailed organic forms that are difficult to achieve with traditional modeling tools.

* **Mudbox** – Mudbox, developed by Autodesk and released in 2007, offers similar digital sculpting functionality. Like ZBrush, it lets artists push, pull, smooth, and shape 3D models using a hands-on sculpting workflow.

* **3DCoat** – 3DCoat, developed by Pilgway, is a 3D software focused on digital sculpting, texture painting, and retopology. It provides artists with a powerful set of tools to create detailed models, paint textures directly onto 3D surfaces, and optimize mesh topology for use in animation and game engines.

* **Marvelous Designer** – Marvelous Designer, developed by CLO Virtual Fashion, is a 3D garment design and simulation software that lets artists create realistic clothing by replicating traditional pattern-making techniques. It accurately mimics properties like weight, elasticity, and drape, so garments naturally conform to a character's physique and move realistically with every motion. Marvelous Designer is widely used in industries like video game development, film production, and digital fashion.

* **TopoGun** – TopoGun, developed by PixelMachine, is a specialized software focused on retopology (the process of creating clean, efficient, and animation-friendly mesh topology over high-resolution 3D models). It comes packed with both manual and automatic tools to help you do just that. On top of that, it's got some solid baking features, too, including one-pass baking for multiple maps and GPU-accelerated ambient occlusion to speed things up.

* **RizomUV** – RizomUV, developed by Rizom-Lab, is a specialized software designed for UV mapping and unwrapping 3D models (the process of flattening a 3D surface into a 2D layout so textures can wrap around models accurately), which is an essential step in 3D asset creation. Known for it's precision and user-friendly interface, RizomUV stands out by offering advanced algorithms that minimize

distortion and maximize texture space. It's widely used alongside other DCC software to streamline the UV and texturing workflow in game and film production.

- **Substance Painter** – Substance Painter is a 3D painting application developed by Adobe (originally by Allegorithmic) that allows artists to paint textures directly onto models in real time. It supports features like smart materials, particle brushes, and mask-based workflows, making it especially intuitive for texturing characters, props, and environment assets.
- **Substance Designer** – Substance Designer is a procedural material creation tool, also developed by Adobe (and originally by Allegorithmic). It uses a node-based system to let artists build flexible, procedural materials from the ground up. It's widely used in game and film production for creating tileable, engine-ready materials and textures.
- **Photoshop** – Photoshop is a raster-based image editing software developed by Adobe. It has become the industry standard for digital painting, photo editing, and texture creation. Its layer system, customizable brushes, and filters make it incredibly flexible for a wide range of creative workflows, from concept art to post-production.
- **Illustrator** – Illustrator is a vector graphics editor, also developed by Adobe. It specializes in creating artwork based on mathematical paths rather than pixels, making it ideal for clean, scalable graphics like logos, UI elements, and icons. Illustrator is widely used in graphic design due to its precision, scalability, and integration with other Adobe tools.
- **Marmoset Toolbag** – Marmoset Toolbag is a real-time rendering and lookdev tool developed by Marmoset LLC. It's primarily used to showcase 3D models with advanced lighting setups, material editing, map baking, and the creation of portfolio-ready turntables and beauty shots.

Toolbag includes many rendering features you'd find in game engines, such as physically based rendering (PBR) for accurate materials and lighting, along with high-quality shadows, reflections, and ambient occlusion.

The interface is intuitive, so you can quickly set up and preview your models with dynamic lighting and textures. It's also widely used for texturing, allowing artists to paint directly on their model in real time. On top of that, it includes advanced tools like real-time ray tracing, texture baking, animation support, and more.

- **MotionBuilder** – MotionBuilder is a specialized animation software developed by Autodesk, focused primarily on motion capture and character animation. Originally released as FiLMBOX by Kaydara in 1994, it was later acquired by Alias in 2004 and then by Autodesk in 2006, where it was rebranded as MotionBuilder (often called Mobu). It also introduced the FBX file format (which comes from its original name, FiLMBOX) and is now an industry standard for swapping 3D files between software.

- **Houdini** – Houdini, developed by SideFX (Side Effects Software), is a powerhouse in the 3D world known for its procedural approach to modeling and animation. Need a forest that grows differently every time? Or a city that builds itself? Houdini can do that. It's like the illusionist, except this one uses nodes instead of spells.

  It's all thanks to its procedural, node-based workflow, which gives you control without locking you into one version of anything.

  And that's not all; it's also widely used to create complex VFX simulations like fire, smoke, destruction, and fluid dynamics with great control and flexibility.

  Once you start digging into it, you'll see why so many technical and VFX artists swear by it.

- **Cinema 4D** – Cinema 4D is a 3D software developed by Maxon. While it's not as commonly used for creating in-game assets like characters or environments, it plays a major role in the games industry through motion graphics, cinematic trailers, and UI/UX animations.

  If you're interested in making games look amazing beyond gameplay – through promotional videos, animated interfaces, or cinematic storytelling – Cinema 4D could be a great tool to add to your skill set.

- **PureRef** – PureRef is a lightweight reference image organizer developed by Idyllic Pixel. If you've ever found yourself juggling a dozen reference images across different windows, this one's for you. It gives you an infinite canvas where you can drag, drop, rotate, resize, and arrange your reference images exactly how you like. No clutter. No distractions. Just your visual library, all in one place.

  You can keep the window floating on top of everything else or lower its opacity if you want to trace or study shapes (super handy). It even lets you sample colors right off the board or leave yourself useful notes.

  Best of all, it's lightweight and runs on Windows, macOS, and Linux. And here's the cherry on top: PureRef is free to use with an optional donation to support its development.

13.9.5 Licensing

Before jumping into any software, there's one thing we need to clear up: software licensing. If you're enrolled as a student, you'll likely have access to cheap or even free student licenses. Great for practice, but they're strictly for learning, not for commercial use.

If you work at a studio, they'll provide the licenses for the software you'll be using. Always stick to approved versions – no cracked or pirated software. Using unauthorized versions risks legal trouble and security issues and can seriously damage your career.

When freelancing or selling work, you need your own commercial licenses. It sounds obvious, but you'd be surprised how many skip this early on. I get it – some of these programs are extremely pricey, and the idea of cracked software might cross your mind. Please don't. Doing so can damage your credibility, violate legal agreements, and create problems if you ever collaborate with studios or clients. I've seen it firsthand – a freelancer used pirated software, and the files they delivered to a client were infected with malware. Mistakes like that can burn bridges quickly, and no one wants that.

Here's a secret that holds true for many: investing in your own license often motivates you to dive deeper and get your money's worth, which can help you learn faster and more effectively. So, stick with legit software – it's a solid step toward becoming a professional and keeps your reputation (and computer) safe.

13.10 POLICIES AND AGREEMENTS

Let's wrap up this chapter with a look at studio policies and legal agreements. Every studio runs a bit differently, with its own set of rules and guidelines that shape how you work and what's expected of you. Understanding these policies isn't just about following the rules but also about protecting yourself as you navigate your career.

13.10.1 Probation Period

Starting a new job? Chances are, you'll hit a probation period first. It's basically a trial run for both you and the studio to see if this role is the right fit. Usually, it lasts three to six months, with three months being the most common.

During this time, you'll get comfortable with the workflow, work along-side your team, and prove what you bring to the table. The workload might start light, but expect it to ramp up as you settle in.

Your performance will be evaluated by your ability to meet deadlines, work well with the team, and prove your value to the studio.

At the end, the studio might confirm your spot, extend probation if they want to see more growth before fully bringing you on, or, in rare cases, let you go if expectations aren't met. If you get an extension, take it seriously – listen to feedback, refine your skills, and show you're willing to grow.

Whatever happens, think of probation as a stepping stone – an opportunity to learn, adapt, and prepare yourself for the role. Most game artists pass with flying colors if they stay focused and committed. Unless you've broken your NDA, underperformed, acted unprofessionally, or – say – intentionally set the office on fire, you're probably in the clear.

13.10.2 Non-disclosure Agreement

We already touched on NDAs back in Chapter 10, but since they're extremely common in the game industry – and apply to your work both on and off the clock – it's worth a quick reminder here.

NDAs are legal contracts designed to protect a company's confidential information and ideas. By signing one, you agree not to share any private details about projects or company secrets. These agreements can remain in effect long after you've left a job – sometimes for months, even years.

Bottom line: breaking an NDA can seriously hurt your career, so treat them carefully.

13.10.3 Creative Rights

The work you create during your job typically belongs to the company. This includes art, concepts, and assets made for projects. Sometimes, even personal or spare-time work can fall under company ownership, depending on your contract.

Remember, video games are commercial products, and studios protect their intellectual property (IP) closely. Using unlicensed or copyrighted materials – like images directly from Google – can cause serious legal trouble. It might seem harmless to add a popular movie logo to your model or use the first texture you find online, but that risks copyright infringement. Some databases offer copyright-free content, but always check usage rights and double-check with your lead, producer, or legal team before incorporating anything into your work.

To stay safe, only use assets owned by the company, properly licensed, or in the public domain. Respecting IP laws and company policies protects you legally and helps keep your reputation strong in the industry.

13.10.4 Non-compete Clause

A non-compete clause usually limits your ability to work with direct competitors, freelance for similar companies, or launch something that competes with your employer. But it can go further: restricting who you work with, the projects you take on, or even how you promote your work publicly. Sometimes, even personal projects could fall under this umbrella if they're in a similar space.

It's a way companies protect their ideas and assets. Makes sense, but for creatives, it can feel pretty restrictive.

And if you violate it? Well, it can get ugly. Legal trouble, financial penalties, or damage to your reputation. Definitely not worth the risk.

So if you're thinking about a side gig or personal project that might conflict with your contract, check with your studio's legal team first. It's always better to be clear than to make assumptions and get into trouble later.

Also, don't forget the "cooling-off" period after leaving a company. That's the time window where the restrictions may still apply. Once that's over, you're usually free to move on and explore new opportunities.

NOTE

1 Binary files are files that store data in a format that's not plain text – so, computers read them as a series of 0s and 1s rather than letters or numbers you can easily read.

Taking Care of Yourself

14

Taking care of yourself might sound like a no-brainer, but it's one of those things that's often overlooked. I know how easy it is to get caught up in deadlines, long hours, and the constant pressure to deliver – often at the expense of your physical, mental, and emotional well-being. Over time, neglecting self-care can lead to burnout, loss of motivation, and a decline in the quality of your work. The truth is, looking after yourself is one of the best investments you can make – for both your career and your health. So, let's talk about how to take care of the most important person behind the art: you.

14.1 DISCLAIMER

Real quick, before we dive in: I'm by no means a trained medical professional. Everything I'm sharing in this chapter is based on personal experience and general knowledge. If you have concerns about your health, I strongly advise reaching out to someone qualified. They're the real experts, and you deserve the best care.

14.2 OVERTIME

Overtime (or often referred to as "crunch") is an unfortunate reality in game development, particularly when deadlines are tight or a project is nearing completion. You've likely heard the term or maybe even lived through it yourself.

And it's not a rare case. Figure 14.1 shows findings provided by Safe In Our World, a mental health charity focused on the games industry, which were featured in Skillsearch's 2024/25 *Games & Interactive Salary & Satisfaction Survey*. Safe In Our World was kind enough to allow me to include these data in the book. The results highlight that a significant number of game developers have experienced crunch firsthand.

Sometimes, it means pulling a late night or working through the weekend to hit a milestone. Other times, it's days of nonstop pressure that slowly wear you down. And while going the extra mile can feel like you're showing commitment, there's a fine line between dedication and burnout.

Overtime should be a choice and never a given. You shouldn't feel obligated to accept it just because someone overpromised or a project was mismanaged. When staying late becomes the norm – when people feel expected to sacrifice evenings and weekends just to keep up – that's when things go sideways.

And while you can't always control the project, you can control how you approach it:

- **Know Your Limits:** familiarize yourself with local overtime regulations (for instance, in both the United Kingdom and the EU, the average legal limit of working time is 48 hours, including overtime). These aren't arbitrary rules; they're there to protect you.
- **Speak Up:** if you're constantly overworked, don't hesitate to speak up – whether that's with HR or your lead.
- **Plan for Downtime:** your health matters more than any deadline. Always make self-care a priority. Whether it's taking short breaks during the day, setting strict boundaries on your work hours, or finding a hobby that helps you unwind.
- **Evaluate Your Choices:** when job hunting, do your research. Check out reviews on websites like Glassdoor or ask directly in interviews about the studio's approach toward overtime and work–life balance. Know what you're signing up for. Find a studio that actually values a healthy work–life balance and stands against crunch culture.

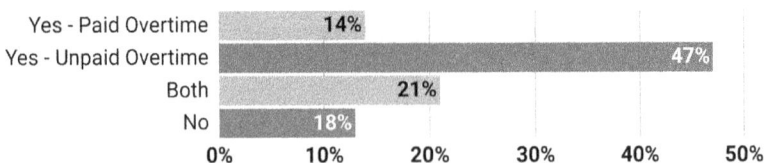

FIGURE 14.1   Percentage of game developers who have experienced crunch.

Source: Based on data from Safe In Our World, featured in Skillsearch's 2024/25 Salary & Satisfaction Survey, used with permission.

So, is overtime always bad? Not necessarily. Sometimes, a short sprint is part of shipping a great project – and if it's paid, optional, and well-managed, it can even be rewarding.

The main factor here is choice. You have every right to look after yourself. In fact, the best work often comes from artists who are well-rested, balanced, and in it for the long run. You're here to make great art, not to burn yourself out in the process.

14.3 BURNOUT

Burnout is the feeling of being drained, both creatively and physically, to the point where you're no longer able to perform at your usual level. It's not being tired after a long day or week; it's an ongoing, cumulative effect of constant stress and pressure over time until you're completely worn out. Think of it like a fire that's burning brightly at first, but eventually, it runs out of fuel and extinguishes itself (hence the name, burnout). In a creative context, burnout happens when you no longer feel inspired, productive, or motivated, no matter how hard you try.

Burnout doesn't happen overnight. It's a gradual decline that starts with small feelings of fatigue or dissatisfaction. At first, you might brush it off, telling yourself, "It's just a bad day." But as the days turn into weeks, the sense of being mentally and physically drained becomes more frequent.

One of the first signs is when your creativity stalls. Ideas won't come. Work that once excited you now feels like a chore. Physically, you may feel tired all the time, get headaches, or notice changes in sleep or appetite. Mentally, you might feel anxious, frustrated, or easily irritated. You may stop caring about deadlines, and your work suffers even though you know you can do better. Emotionally, small problems feel huge, and you might become overly sensitive to criticism or short-tempered with others.

If you want to keep burnout at bay, it's important to take steps to prevent it:

- **Take Breaks and Disconnect**: regular breaks are a must. Step away from work for short periods, and take longer breaks to fully disconnect from work.
- **Set Boundaries and Avoid Overworking**: your worth isn't tied to the number of hours you work. Set limits to avoid late nights or weekend work. Overworking only hurts your productivity and well-being.

- **Focus on Small Wins**: breaking your tasks into smaller, manageable steps will help build momentum and give you that sense of achievement.
- **Take Care of Your Body and Mind**: keep active, eat well, and make sure you're getting enough sleep. Find activities that help recharge you, whether it's gaming, reading, sports, or hanging out with family or friends.
- **Leverage Support Systems**: reach out to someone you trust – friends, family, a mentor, or a dedicated professional – for guidance and support. Also, many companies offer mental and physical health resources, so check with HR to see what's available.

Even with precautions, burnout can still happen. If you're running on empty, don't ignore it. Step back, take a breather, and give yourself the space to recover.

14.4 MENTAL HEALTH

Safe In Our World also shared findings in Skillsearch's *Games & Interactive Salary & Satisfaction Survey* of 2024/25, where 43% of respondents said they struggled with poor mental health in the last year (Figure 14.2). That's almost half. I'm sharing that not to scare you but to remind you that if you're feeling off, overwhelmed, or just not yourself, you're not alone. This is real. It's common. And it's okay to ask for help.

Think of your energy like a jar. Your focus, creativity, and emotional bandwidth all draw from the same jar. Every time you do something that recharges you – a walk, a hobby, sports, and time with family and friends – you're filling it. But when it's empty? Your creativity and focus take a hit because you can't pour from an empty jar, so make sure you're regularly refilling it.

One way to keep that jar from running low could be through journaling. When you're feeling overwhelmed or stuck, take a few minutes to write things out. Don't worry – you don't need to write a novel. Even writing down a few quick thoughts or a simple to-do list can help you process what's on your mind and ease the stress. Remember back in Chapter 1 when we talked about writing down your career action plan? This is a similar idea. Putting things into words helps lighten the mental load. It's a simple practice, but it works.

Mindfulness can help too. Taking a few minutes each day – whether it's through meditation, focusing on your breath, or enjoying a well-deserved relaxing bath – can help you slow down, clear your head, and reduce anxiety. (Just don't overdo the baths, or you might end up like a raisin.)

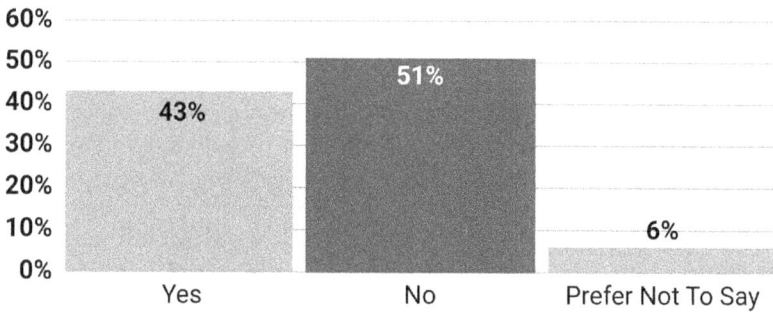

FIGURE 14.2 Percentage of game industry professionals who reported poor mental health in 2024.

Source: Based on data from Safe In Our World, featured in Skillsearch's 2024/25 Salary & Satisfaction Survey, used with permission.

Personally, walking and swimming are my go-to ways to clear my head. Walking gives me a break from screens and helps me reset. Swimming, on the other hand, lets me dive (literally) into a quiet space where I can turn inward without distractions. Like those "shower thoughts," it's often where my best ideas show up.

At the end of the day, your mental health is just as important as your physical health. And while good self-care can go a long way, sometimes it's not enough on its own. If you're feeling stuck or need someone to talk to, reach out – whether it's to someone you trust or a dedicated professional. There's absolutely no shame in asking for help. It's a step toward taking care of yourself, not a sign of weakness. For additional support, see the list of organizations provided at the end of this chapter. Don't wait. Help is always available.

14.5 PHYSICAL HEALTH

Working in games often means long hours in front of a screen, sitting for ages – habits that can take a toll on your body over time. Most of us don't expect to deal with wrist pain, stiff necks, or aching backs when we start out. We love what we do, so it's easy to get lost in the flow and forget to move. But the truth is, your body keeps score, and eventually, it'll make sure you feel it.

I learned this the hard way. About five years ago, I pushed myself too hard to finish a project before a deadline, even though my body was already warning me. The result? Tennis elbow – both arms. Apparently, my body thought, "Why not double the fun?" For those who don't know, tennis elbow is a repetitive strain injury that causes pain on the outside of your elbow from overusing your forearm muscles. It flares up randomly and is a constant reminder that I need to pay attention to my body.

And I'm far from the only one. Many people in the industry experience repetitive strain issues – from wrists and elbows to back pain, headaches, and eye fatigue. A former colleague of mine even had to undergo surgery for a herniated disc from years of poor posture. So seriously, trust me on this one: don't ignore the signals your body's sending.

The good news is that taking care of your physical health doesn't have to be this big, intimidating thing. You don't need to be an athlete or follow a strict diet. Just move more if you sit most of the day. Even small stuff, like walking up a few flights of stairs instead of taking the elevator, adds up.

Stretching is a simple way to stay flexible and fight off aches from sitting. Just a few quick desk stretches or short daily routines away from your chair can make a noticeable difference. They ease muscle tension and can help you relax.

Massage can also help if you're stiff or sore. It might hurt a bit at first, but afterward, that nagging pain often eases. The goal is to keep your body mobile and pain-free for the long haul.

Now, I know some of this sounds like common sense – eat well, drink water, and get enough sleep. But when you're caught up in work, it's easy to forget the basics. Even mild dehydration can affect your focus and energy. If the snacks at work aren't the healthiest, consider asking for better options or bringing your own. Aim for balanced meals with protein, healthy fats, and fiber.

Sleep is just as important. Pulling all-nighters might seem productive, but running on little sleep will tank your energy, creativity, and mood. Aim for seven to eight hours of sleep when you can.

Finally, get outside. Swap pixels for fresh air and daylight. Even ten minutes away from the screen can reset your brain.

The game industry demands a lot, so take care of your body that is doing the work. Stretch. Hydrate. Move. Sleep. Step outside. Small habits, big payoff. Your body will thank you for it.

14.5.1 Ergonomics

Ergonomics – you've heard the word, but what's it about? At its core, it's the art of setting up your workspace to work with your body, not the other way around.

The term comes from the Greek words *ergon* (meaning "work") and *nomos* (meaning "law" or "knowledge"). So, when we put them together, it's essentially "the knowledge of work," and that's exactly what it is: knowing how to make your workspace and habits work *for* you.

Think of it this way: your environment should support you, not strain you. If your workspace isn't set up properly, your body ends up paying the price. Poor ergonomics can lead to serious, long-term issues like carpal tunnel, tendonitis, back and neck pain, and eye strain – all common among artists and anyone glued to a desk for hours. These injuries build up slowly but can leave a lasting impact if you don't catch them early. That's why it's worth setting things up in ways that keep your body comfortable and free from unnecessary stress.

Start with the basics. Position your monitor at eye level so your neck doesn't get sore. Keep your keyboard, mouse, and tablet within easy reach so you're not stretching or twisting awkwardly. Organize your workspace so the tools you use most are within easy reach. These small adjustments can make a big difference over time.

Furniture matters, too. If you're working from home, a proper, adjustable chair that supports your back is one of the best investments you can make. A sit-stand desk can also help break up the day, improve circulation, and reduce fatigue. More and more studios are catching on to this, and many now offer ergonomic setups to support healthier, more sustainable work environments.

Don't overlook comfort, either. If your workspace is cold, your muscles tend to tense up, which can lead to stiffness and increase the risk of strain. So, keep warm – turn on the heating or throw on a hoodie, some cozy socks, or fingerless gloves if needed.

Lighting also plays a role. If possible, position your desk near a window, but avoid placing light sources directly in front of or behind your screen. Glare and high contrast can strain your eyes. If your eyes still feel tired, you can try blue-light filtering glasses. Alternatively, the built-in *Night Light* app on Windows adds a warm color filter to your screen to reduce harsh screen light, making it easier on your eyes – especially at night when your room is dark. Just keep in mind that both options can alter color accuracy, which may be an issue for color-sensitive work like texturing, painting, or design.

And here's the big one: take breaks. Even the best setup won't help if you stay frozen in one position. Step away, stretch, and rest your eyes. Short, regular breaks are like hitting the reset button on both your body and your mind.

Of course, there's a lot more to ergonomics than I can cover here – entire careers are built around understanding it. But if you take even a few of these ideas and put them into practice, you'll already be doing your body a big favor.

14.6 IMPOSTOR SYNDROME

If you've ever thought, "I don't deserve to be here," or "Everyone else is way ahead of me," you're not alone. These feelings don't reflect your abilities, but they're just a distorted version of how you see yourself.

It's that persistent feeling that you don't belong, that others are more talented, that you're somehow just "faking it," and sooner or later, someone's going to find out. Yes, that one. But the truth is, even the most seasoned professionals have these doubts. The key is learning how to manage it so it doesn't hold you back.

Growing as an artist means making mistakes, facing challenges, and pushing beyond your comfort zone. Feeling uncomfortable isn't a sign of incompetence; it's proof you're growing.

So, when impostor syndrome starts creeping in, here's what you can do to push back:

- **Keep track of your wins:** finished a project you're proud of? Got a compliment from someone you respect? Landed your first job? Save those moments. Keep a folder, a journal – whatever works for you. On tough days, looking back at your progress can be a powerful reminder of how far you've come.
- **Let go of perfectionism:** perfectionism and impostor syndrome go hand in hand. It makes you believe that anything less than flawless isn't good enough. But no one, not even the best ones out there, produces perfect work every time.
- **Stop comparing yourself to others:** scrolling through portfolios or social media can make you feel like you're falling behind, but the only person you should compare yourself to is your past self. Focus on how much you've improved – that's what really counts.
- **Talk about it:** you'd be surprised how many artists feel this way but keep it quiet. Sharing helps take away the power of self-doubt.
- **Accept that you don't need to know everything:** the best artists keep learning, ask questions, and aren't afraid to try new things.
- **Keep going:** the more you create, the more confident you get. Over time, impostor syndrome loses its grip.

Impostor syndrome doesn't get to decide your worth. You earned your opportunities through skill, potential, and hard work. You are more than capable. Believe in yourself.

14.7 CREATIVE BLOCKS

Creative blocks are frustrating but bound to happen. After all, you're not a machine. I mean, I'm pretty sure even R2-D2 needs a recharge now and then. Hitting a wall doesn't mean you've lost your touch. Usually, they come from burnout, lack of inspiration, or overthinking. Often, they're temporary, but if ignored, they can stick around for much longer than you'd like. Feeling stuck is just part of the process, and it's important to know when to take a break and reset.

So, how do you break out of it? Sometimes, a simple change of scenery helps. When I was writing this book, I'd head to a local cat café with my tablet, or take printed pages to the park to proofread. Shifting your environment – even if it's just moving your desk or working from a different corner of the room – can refresh your perspective and spark new ideas. Remember how exciting it felt as a kid to rearrange your room or move into a new one? That same sense of novelty can still boost your creativity as an adult.

If that's not enough, try narrowing your focus. Breaking your work into bite-sized pieces makes it manageable and helps you build momentum. Or, set creative limits: use just one color, one brush, or one tool. Forget the pressure to "perform" and just play with ideas. Creativity thrives when you give yourself room to experiment.

Sometimes, the best move is stepping away altogether. Take a walk, go for a swim, or build a LEGO set – whatever gets you out of your head. When you come back, you're looking at the same problem but from a new angle. And that's often when things start to click.

> *"When you think you're done or feel like what you're producing is garbage, walk away from what you're working on for at least 30 minutes. Then come back and look at your stuff with new eyes."*
>
> – Oliver Elm

14.8 EXTERNAL ORGANIZATIONS

I want to take a moment to highlight some incredible organizations doing very important work around mental and physical health for those in the games industry.

But before we get to the list, it's worth repeating that there's absolutely no shame in reaching out for help. None. In fact, asking for help is a sign of self-awareness and strength. And if the idea of speaking up feels intimidating, don't worry – most (if not all) of these organizations offer anonymous support. You're not alone, and there's always a safe, confidential way to get the help you need.

Also, don't forget that many studios partner with external organizations to support your well-being. Be sure to find out what resources your studio offers. It's well worth knowing what's available to you.

- **Healthy Gamer:** Healthy Gamer offers coaching and mental health resources tailored for gamers and developers, with a focus on burnout, stress, and overall well-being.
- **International Game Developers Association (IGDA):** IGDA is the largest global network of game creators, offering mental health and work-life resources through its Mental Health Special Interest Group (SIG).
- **Safe In Our World:** Safe In Our World is a games industry charity focused on reducing stigma and supporting mental health through training, toolkits, and awareness campaigns.
- **Take This:** Take This is a US-based nonprofit promoting mental health in gaming. They provide educational resources, crisis support, and training for developers and players.
- **The Game Developers Conference (GDC) – Health & Wellness Events:** the GDC features wellness sessions such as meditation, yoga, and talks on stress and burnout, supporting both the physical and mental health of attendees.
- **The International Games Summit on Mental Health (TIGS):** TIGS is an annual event where industry professionals and mental health experts gather for panels and discussions on well-being in games.

What's Next?　15

As you progress through your career, it's important to look ahead and ask yourself, "What's next?" As your skills grow, so too will your goals, interests, and opportunities. Maybe you're aiming for a promotion, transitioning to another role, or considering leaving the industry entirely. Whatever the case, understanding how to navigate these shifts is important.

15.1 CAREER PROGRESSION

You've already seen how roles like junior, mid-level, senior, principal, and lead fit into the structure of a typical game art career. But career progression isn't just about titles. It's about figuring out what kind of work keeps you engaged and what kind of growth matters to you.

In the beginning, your focus is on learning: how teams work, how pipelines function, and how to collaborate and deliver. Over time, your responsibilities grow – maybe that means mentoring, owning parts of the pipeline, or shaping a visual direction. Eventually, you might step into leadership roles. Or not. Some people love managing teams; others prefer staying close to the craft. Roles like principal artist exist for that very reason.

The truth is, there's no one path. You don't have to follow anyone else's template. I've seen people move up, shift sideways, change disciplines, or even leave the industry entirely. What matters most is that you check in with yourself regularly. What drives you now? What do you want to learn next? Your goals will evolve, and your career should evolve with them. Keep pushing yourself, stay curious, and learn new tools and techniques. Set clear goals for yourself and stay open to new opportunities that align with your evolving interests and aspirations, especially in a fast-moving industry like this one.

DOI: 10.1201/9781003492320-15

15.2 MOVING ON

At some point, you'll probably hit a moment in your career where you feel the itch for something new. You've been on the same project for what feels like forever, and the excitement starts to fade. If you're starting to feel like there's nothing more for you to learn or you're simply bored, that could be a sign to think about moving on. That could mean stepping into a new role, redefining your responsibilities, or making the leap to a different company. It's common for developers to jump between studios to gain new experiences, work on bigger projects, or increase their visibility and income.

According to Skillsearch's *Games & Interactive Salary & Satisfaction Survey* of 2024/25, 77% of respondents were or are thinking about job hunting. Yes, that's a big chunk of people on the move or at least considering it.

Additionally, 39% said they'd be open to switching to a completely different discipline within art. That shows just how many creatives are ready to try something new and shake things up – and it might help you see that, when you're feeling stuck, moving on can sometimes be the best decision you make to keep pushing your career forward.

Of course, companies know this and might try to pull you back with a raise or additional perks if they see you eyeing the door. But honestly, while that can be tempting, it's not always enough if you're already set on moving forward.

Not sure if it's time to move on? Here are a few signs that might mean it's time to consider the next chapter in your career:

- You're doing the same things day in and day out, and it feels like you're just spinning your wheels.
- You no longer feel that thrill or stretch from tackling new challenges.
- You're ready for new challenges, but they're nowhere in sight.
- Your vision is bigger than what your current role can support.
- Your performance reviews have become predictable and unhelpful.
- You've grown, but your paycheck hasn't.

It's absolutely normal to have doubts when contemplating a career change, even if you've been in the industry for years. Though change can be intimidating, it's often the right step for your personal and professional growth. Staying in a job that doesn't push you anymore is essentially choosing to stay stuck. Of course, this ultimately varies per individual; if you're genuinely content with where you are, there's nothing wrong with that. Just keep in mind that without continued growth or initiative, promotions and raises are unlikely to appear out of nowhere.

15.2.1 Exit Strategy

Thinking about leaving your job? How you go about it matters more than you might think. It's not just about handing in your resignation and walking out the door; it's about preserving good professional connections. You never know when you'll cross paths with former colleagues again or even return to a previous workplace. Leaving on good terms protects your reputation and keeps doors open for the future.

Before you resign, here are some things to keep in mind:

- **Secure Your Next Move**: Ideally, you want to have your next role lined up before you hand in your resignation. This ensures you're not jumping into uncertainty.
- **Notice Period**: Most companies require one to three months' notice. This helps with a smooth handover and finding your replacement. Sometimes, when everyone agrees, you could leave earlier – so don't be afraid to ask.
- **Keep it Quiet (For Now)**: Hold off on telling coworkers until your resignation is official. Early gossip can create tension you don't need.
- **Talk to Your Manager or Lead**: If you've built a good relationship with your manager or lead, have a face-to-face conversation to let them know you're thinking of leaving. It's a respectful move and gives them the chance to discuss your decision openly.

Once you've made it official, focus on leaving well:

- **Avoid Negativity**: Don't badmouth your colleagues or the company. It hurts your reputation and can come back to you later.
- **Send a Farewell Note**: A short, positive farewell message is a thoughtful way to thank your team and leave on a good note. Many also include their contact info to make it easier for others to stay in touch.
- **Wrap Up Thoughtfully**: Finish your work, organize files, and leave notes or documentation for whoever takes over. Clean your workspace and return any company gear in good shape.

Feeling unsure about leaving is normal. Growth happens when you step out of your comfort zone, challenge yourself, and learn new things. Staying stuck might feel safe, but it can hold you back. Change might just be exactly what you need.

15.3 CONTINUING TO GROW

Austin Kleon said it best in his book *Keep Going*: "No matter how success-ful you get, no matter what level of achievement you reach, you will never really *arrive*. Other than death, there is no finish line or retirement for the creative person."[1] It's true. The moment you think you've "arrived," there's always something new waiting to be learned, a skill to sharpen, or a fresh idea to explore. That's the nature of a creative career. It never stops evolving.

The artists who stand out aren't the ones who settle. They're the ones who keep pushing, staying curious, resilient, and adaptable. Growth isn't just about improving your art; it's about building a mindset that embraces change and challenges.

The creative world moves fast. New software, tools, and workflows keep popping up. If something feels outdated or slows you down, don't be afraid to let it go and pick up something new. That said, some long-standing tools and workflows have stuck around for a reason – they work, and learning them is never wasted time. Most skills transfer across tools anyway, so you're always investing in your future.

And while tools change, the fundamentals of art don't. Mastering basics like composition, color, anatomy, and lighting will strengthen your foundation, no matter what tools you use. Even if you mostly work digitally, brushing up on traditional techniques will sharpen your eye and level up your work.

Don't get stuck doing things one way. Try new workflows, experiment with styles, and take on personal projects that stretch you. You'll fail some-times, and that's a good thing. Failure means you're trying, learning, and growing. Worst case, you figure out what doesn't work. Best case, you unlock something amazing that pushes your art further.

At the same time, be ambitious and set goals for yourself. Want to learn a new tool? Improve your speed? Build a killer portfolio piece? Break your goals down into smaller steps and celebrate every win, no matter how small. Every bit of progress counts.

And here's a big one we did touch on before: don't shy away from feed-back. Ask for it, listen closely, and use it to improve. The best artists don't accept criticism; they seek it out.

Remember, becoming a skilled game artist takes time. It's easy to look at top artists and feel like you'll never get there, but don't forget, they were all once beginners, too. It's the result of years of practice, dedication, and a genu-ine passion for learning the craft. Talent helps, but dedication is what really separates the good from the great.

> *"In this fast-moving industry, staying curious is your superpower. Treat every challenge as a chance to grow; the problems that frustrate you today will be the skills that define you tomorrow."*
>
> – Mohsen Tabasi

NOTE

1 Austin Kleon, *Keep Going: 10 Ways to Stay Creative in Good Times and Bad* (New York: Workman Publishing, 2019), 10.

Closing Words

And just like that, we've reached the end. If you've made it this far, a huge thank you – I'm grateful you chose to read this book all the way through.

We've covered a lot together, and I hope you've learned something valuable along the way. As you step forward in your journey as a game artist, remember that it's a journey full of ups and downs. When things get tough, see it as a chance to level up your skills. Keep pushing boundaries, believe in what you do, and enjoy every moment of turning your passion into a fulfilling career.

If you found this book helpful, I'd be grateful if you spread the word with others, recommend it to a friend, or consider leaving a review online. And if you just want to say hi or let me know what you thought, I'd love to hear from you. You can contact me anytime through my website or socials. I do my best to reply to everyone, though I may not always be able to. That said, every message is genuinely appreciated and means a lot.

That's all from me for now. Wishing you all the best in your career, and I hope to see you out there.

– Sander
https://sanderflisijn.com/

For Product Safety Concerns and Information please contact our EU
representative GPSR@taylorandfrancis.com
Taylor & Francis Verlag GmbH, Kaufingerstraße 24, 80331 München, Germany